Essential GCSE Latin

Essential GCSE Latin

John Taylor

Bristol Classical Press

Published by Bristol Classical Press 2012

Bristol Classical Press, an imprint of Bloomsbury Publishing Plc

Bloomsbury Publishing Plc
50 Bedford Square
London WC1B 3DP
www.bloomsburyacademic.com

Copyright © John Taylor 2006

First published by Gerald Duckworth & Co. Ltd. 2006

The author has asserted his rights under the Copyright, Designs and
Patents Act 1988 to be identified as the author of this work.

ISBN: 978 1 85399 693 1

A CIP catalogue record for this book is available from the British Library

Typeset by John Taylor
Printed and bound in Great Britain by the MPG Books Group, Bodmin, Cornwall

Contents

Contents

Preface

This book is a summary of all the linguistic requirements for GCSE Latin (OCR specification, 2007 onwards). It is neither a complete course from scratch nor a traditional reference grammar (though it could at a pinch be used as either). It is aimed mainly at pupils in their GCSE year, though I hope it may also have a use in other contexts where the threads of previous study need to be pulled together (for scholarship preparation, or after transfer to a new school or a new teacher). Whatever course pupils have used, many remain very hazy about grammar. It is difficult to track back in a multi-volume course to the first introduction of a particular construction. Traditional grammars on the other hand can be forbidding, and often do not give enough help with syntax and idiom. This book breaks everything down into bite-sized chunks, with examples and practice sentences (650 in all) on each point. There is some deliberate repetition, but much more use of cross-referencing. The treatment is not purely sequential (sentences testing nouns have to include verbs), but complications irrelevant to the point under discussion have as far as possible been avoided. *Essential GCSE Latin* concentrates on the understanding of principles, both in the formation of words and in the construction of sentences, in order to cut down on rote learning. Every year examiners' reports comment that many candidates muddle through translation and comprehension passages with too little attention to grammar: endings are ignored, and common constructions not recognised. This book is an invitation to take grammar seriously and to understand its basic terminology.

All the examples and most of the practice sentences are confined to the Defined Vocabulary List of about 450 words prescribed by OCR for the GCSE Paper 1 Momentum Test. Exercises of this type (combining comprehension and unseen translation) are provided by Ashley Carter in *Latin Momentum Tests for GCSE* (Bristol Classical Press 2003), to which this book is intended to be complementary. The fifteen translation passages included here are intended as practice for the optional harder unseen (Paper 3) and assume knowledge of the supplementary Defined Vocabulary List of about 130 words. This additional list is also sometimes referred to in other connections. The vocabulary in the back of this book is an aggregate of the two lists. I have not made special provision for Foundation Tier, though where practicable I have had an eye on its reduced vocabulary in choosing examples. To save space a default system operates in the description of grammar (a verb is active unless specified as passive, indicative unless specified as subjunctive).

I happily acknowledge a debt (particularly in the Glossary of grammar terms) to James Morwood *A Latin Grammar* (Oxford University Press 1999), to which I refer any reader who considers my concentration on GCSE requirements to involve excessive economy with the truth.

I am grateful to Deborah Blake and Ray Davies at Duckworth for their helpful guidance.

John Taylor
Tonbridge School

Abbreviations

abl	ablative
acc	accusative
adj	adjective
adv	adverb
conj	conjunction
dat	dative
dep	deponent
f	feminine
gen	genitive
indecl	indeclinable (does not change its endings)
irreg	irregular
m	masculine
n	neuter
nom	nominative
num	numeral
pl	plural
prep	preposition
pron	pronoun
refl	reflexive
s-dep	semi-deponent
sg	singular
usu	usually
voc	vocative
1, 2, 3	first, second, third person; first, second, third etc declension
1st, 2nd, 3rd	first, second, third etc conjugation

Note also two abbreviations of Latin expressions which are common in English, and frequently used in the explanations of grammar in this book:

e.g.	*exempli gratia*	for (the sake of) example
i.e.	*id est*	that is (*introducing further explanation*)

Glossary of grammar terms

ablative	case expressing *by, with, from*; used with prepositions expressing motion away from, or being in a place.
accusative	case of direct object; used with prepositions expressing motion towards; used for subject of infinitive in indirect statement.
active	form of verb where the grammatical subject is the doer of the action (as distinct from passive).
adjective	word describing a noun (with which it agrees in number, gender and case).
adverb	word describing a verb (or an adjective, or another adverb).
agree	have the same number (agreement of subject and verb); have the same number, gender and case (agreement of noun and adjective).
ambiguous	can mean more than one thing.
antecedent	noun or pronoun in main clause to which relative pronoun refers back.
auxiliary	a verb (usually part of *to be*) used with a participle to form a tense of another verb (e.g. perfect passive *portati sumus* = we have been carried).
case	form of a noun, pronoun or adjective that shows the job it does in the sentence (e.g. accusative for direct object); cases are arranged in the order nominative, (vocative), accusative, genitive, dative, ablative.
clause	part of a sentence with its own subject and verb.
comparative	form of an adjective or adverb meaning *more, -er* (e.g. *longior* = longer).
complement	another nominative word or phrase describing the subject.
compound	verb with prefix (e.g. *exire* = to go out).
conditional	clause beginning *if* or *unless*.
conjugate	go through the different parts of a verb (e.g. *porto, portas, portat*).
conjugation	one of the four main patterns by which verbs change their endings.
conjunction	word joining clauses, phrases or words together (e.g. *and, but, therefore*).
consonant	letter representing a sound that can only be used together with a vowel.
construction	pattern according to which a particular type of sentence or clause (e.g. indirect statement) is formed.
dative	case of indirect object, often translated *to* or *for*.
declension	one of the patterns (three main ones, also used for adjectives, and two less common) by which nouns change their endings.
decline	go through the different parts of a noun, pronoun or adjective in case order.
deponent	verb which is passive in form but active in meaning.
defective verb	verb of which only a few parts exist.
direct object	noun or pronoun on receiving end of the action of verb.
direct speech	actual words of a speaker, usually enclosed by inverted commas.
ending	last bit of a word, added to the stem to give more detail and show its job.
feminine	one of the three genders, for females or things imagined as female.
finite	form of a verb with tense and person ending (as distinct from infinitive or participle).
future perfect	tense of verb referring to something that will have happened by a certain point in the future.
future	tense of verb referring to something that will happen in the future.

gender	one of three categories (masculine, feminine, neuter) into which nouns and pronouns are put according to their actual or imagined sex or lack of it.
genitive	case expressing possession or definition, often translated *of*.
gerundive	adjective formed from verb, expressing the idea *needing to be done*.
homonym	word coincidentally spelled in the same way as another unconnected word.
imperative	form of verb used for direct command.
imperfect	tense of verb referring to incomplete, extended or repeated action in the past.
impersonal	third person singular verb whose subject is *it*.
indeclinable	does not change its endings.
indicative	form of verb expressing a fact (usually as distinct from subjunctive).
indirect	indirect statement, command or question is the reported form of it (as distinct from quotation of the speaker's actual words); indirect object is person or thing in the dative indirectly affected by object of verb, e.g. *I gave the money* (direct object) *to the old man* (indirect object).
infinitive	form of verb introduced by *to*, expressing the basic meaning (e.g. *currere* = to run).
intransitive	verb that does not have a direct object (e.g. *festino* = I hurry).
irregular	word that does not follow one of the standard declensions or conjugations.
locative	special case ending of some nouns expressing *at* or *in*.
main clause	clause which makes sense on its own, and expresses the main point of a sentence (as distinct from subordinate clause).
masculine	one of the three genders, for males or things imagined as male.
negative	expressing that something is not the case or should not happen.
neuter	one of the three genders, for things imagined as neither male nor female.
nominative	case used for subject of sentence.
noun	word naming a person or thing (e.g. *urbs* = city; a *proper* noun with a capital letter gives its actual name e.g. *Roma* = Rome).
number	being either singular or plural.
numerals	numbers.
object	noun or pronoun acted upon by a verb.
part of speech	category of word (noun, adjective, pronoun, verb, adverb, preposition, conjunction).
participle	adjective formed from a verb (e.g. *portans* = carrying, *portatus* = having been carried).
passive	form of verb where the subject does not do the action but is on the receiving end of it (e.g. *capior* = I am captured).
perfect	tense of verb referring to a completed action in the past.
person	term for the subject of verb: first person = *I*, *we*; second person = *you*, third person = *he*, *she*, *it*, *they* (or a noun replacing one of these).
phrase	group of words not containing a finite verb (as distinct from clause).
pluperfect	tense of verb referring to something that had already happened by a particular point in the past.
plural	more than one.

possessive	adjective or pronoun expressing who or what something belongs to.
prefix	word or syllable added to the beginning of another word.
preposition	word used with a noun or pronoun in the accusative or ablative to focus more closely the meaning of the case (e.g. *into*).
present	tense of a verb referring to something that is happening now.
principal parts	set of (usually four) parts of a verb from which you can work out all necessary information about it: present tense (first person singular), infinitive, perfect tense (first person singular), perfect passive participle (if the verb has one).
pronoun	word that stands instead of a noun, avoiding the need to repeat it.
reflexive	word referring back to the subject of the verb.
relative	subordinate clause (or pronoun introducing it) relating to person or thing just mentioned in the main clause.
sentence	group of words with subject and verb (and often other elements), which can stand on its own (as distinct from phrase or subordinate clause).
singular	just one (as distinct from plural).
stem	the part of a word which stays the same: different endings are added to show the job it does in the sentence.
subject	noun or pronoun in the nominative case, expressing who or what does the action (with active verb) or is on the receiving end of it (with passive verb).
subjunctive	form of verb referring not to a fact but to an idea or possibility (as distinct from indicative).
subordinate	of secondary importance to something else; a subordinate clause cannot stand alone but only makes sense in relation to the main clause.
superlative	form of adjective or adverb meaning *very, most, -est* (e.g. *altissimus* = very high, highest).
supply	provide in translation a word which is not separately represented in Latin but worked out from the grammar and context (e.g. *multa dixit* = he said many *things*).
syllable	part of a word forming a spoken unit, usually consisting of vowel with consonants before or after or both.
tense	form of a verb showing when the action takes place (in the past, present or future).
transitive	verb that has a direct object.
verb	word expressing an action.
vocative	case used for addressing someone or something.
vowel	letter representing a sound that can be spoken by itself: *a, e, i, o, u, y*.

The importance of word endings

English depends mainly on word order to show what job each word does in a sentence. A simple sentence has the order *subject, verb, object*:

The boy is looking for the girl

Latin behaves in a different way. There are indeed some typical patterns (though they are different from English), so that a simple sentence often has the order *subject, object, verb*:

puer puellam quaerit.
The boy is looking for the girl.

But this is much less important than the word endings. If the word endings and the word order seem to be in conflict, the endings win every time:

puellam puer quaerit.
still means   The boy is looking for the girl.

If you ask why put it in this peculiar order, the answer is for emphasis, to give special stress (in this example) to the accusative word that has been hauled to the front of the sentence:

The boy is looking for *the girl* (*implying* and not someone else).
or   It is the girl the boy is looking for.

In this second translation the grammar of the Latin is modified but the word order is preserved. You can only reverse the *meaning* by swapping the case endings:

puella puerum quaerit.
The girl is looking for the boy.

A recent GCSE unseen translation passage included the following sentence (in direct speech, as an announcement to the crowded Forum in Rome):

proelio magno victi sumus.   (*proelium* = battle)

The heading explained that the story was about the Romans' disastrous defeat in battle by Hannibal at Lake Trasimene in 217 BC. Despite this, and despite the grammar, a large number of candidates wrote something like: *We have won a big battle*. This shows the hazards of simply taking the basic meaning of the words, then trying to create a sentence out of them. Just like failing to apply common sense in squaring the heading with the story, ignoring endings is *failing to use information you have been given*: this accounts for more lost marks in GCSE than anything else. Basic knowledge of endings should have enabled all candidates to spot that *proelio magno* must be dative or ablative (in fact it is ablative), and that *victi sumus* is perfect passive. The correct translation is of course:

We have been defeated in a big battle.

That is what to write for full marks. Note however that the Latin sentence gets its impact from the progressive way in which the news is revealed. Imagine we are Romans in the listening crowd: *proelio* tells us there has been a battle, *magno* that it was a big one, *victi* that some people have been defeated, and *sumus* that those people are us. Because the endings give the basic meaning, the word order is freed up to create other effects. Word endings are neither an optional extra nor a necessary nuisance but the essential means of understanding Latin properly, enjoying it and getting good results. This book aims to help you to use efficiently the information which endings provide.

Nominative case

A *case* is the form of a noun, pronoun or adjective showing the job it does in the sentence. Its name comes from *casus* (= a falling): like *a bad case of measles* (the way events fall out), but not *a good case of wine* (that is a *homonym*). In Latin grammar the other cases are imagined as falling away at increasing angles from the upright purity of the nominative. This also explains the terms *decline* and *declension*: in listing the cases of a particular word in order, you trace the pattern by which they fall away from the vertical.

• Refer to the Glossary (pages ix-xi) for any grammar terms not fully understood.

The nominative is used for the subject of a sentence or clause. The term comes from *nomen,* stem *nomin-* (= name): the nominative *names* the person or thing the sentence is going to be about. In a typical sentence with an active verb, it refers to the person who does the action:

> servus murum aedificat.
> <u>The slave</u> builds the wall.

Regular nominative endings for the three main declensions:

	first	*second*	*third*
sg	-a	-us (-um *if n*)	(*wide range of possibilities*)
pl	-ae	-i (-a *if n*)	-es (-a *if n*)

• See full tables of noun declensions: pages 9-15.

A singular subject must have a singular verb: noun and verb must *agree* in number. Two singulars make a plural:

> puer et puella per viam ambulabant.
> The boy and the girl were walking along the street.

A nominative word very frequently begins a sentence. If a sentence does not start with a nominative, the subject of the verb usually has to be worked out from the verb ending:

> clamorem audivimus.
> We heard a shout.

The verb can tell you if the subject is third person, but cannot by itself tell you who it refers to. When a third person verb has no subject expressed, you normally assume the subject is the same as that of the previous sentence:

> servus cibum abstulit. deinde e villa fugit.
> The slave stole the food. Then he fled from the house.

Less commonly, a nominative word may be in the sentence, but postponed in order to put another word first for emphasis (first and last in the sentence are the strongest positions for this purpose):

cibum servus abstulit, non pecuniam.
The slave stole *food* (*or* It was *food* the slave stole), not *money*.

Another noun or descriptive phrase referring to the subject is also nominative:

miles, vir ingens, ianuam facile fregit.
The soldier, a huge man, easily broke the door.

A second nominative also follows the verb *to be*:

frater meus nauta est.
My brother is a sailor.

The second noun here is called the *complement*. Contrast this with the accusative object:

frater meus nautam adiuvit.
My brother helped the sailor.

The nominative is quoted as the basic form of a noun (or adjective or pronoun), but it is not simply a default case. A word can only be nominative if it is the subject of a *finite* verb, i.e. a verb with a tense and a person ending. Any sentence contains or implies a nominative as the subject of the main verb. A complex sentence can include one or more *additional* nominatives (each the subject of a subordinate clause) if it meets this requirement:

cum amici advenissent, adeo risimus ut senex iratus esset.
When <u>our friends</u> had arrived, <u>we</u> laughed so much that <u>the old man</u> was angry.

This rule explains why in an indirect statement the subject of the infinitive is accusative (see page 92). In general a Latin word which does not qualify as nominative is likely to be accusative or ablative (see pages 87-9 on ablative absolute).

Note that in a passage proper names (usually given underneath, with grammar details) need to be *put back into the nominative* in translation:

omnes Caesarem salutavimus.
We all greeted Caesar.

Vocative case

This is used to address or speak directly to someone. Its name comes from *voco* (= I call). Older books list it separately after the nominative when they set out noun declensions, making six cases rather than five. It is now normally just shown as a footnote where necessary: the vocative is the same as the nominative for most singulars and all plurals (and applies only to nouns and adjectives, not pronouns).

The main distinctive vocative form to note is the ending *-e* for second declension masculine nouns (see page 10):

sg	*nom*	domin-us
	voc	domin-e

• Note that *filius* (= son) drops the *-e*, so that its vocative is *fili*.

A vocative is usually easy to spot in a sentence. It is often separated off by a comma or commas. It is often found together with an imperative (see page 71). It is even easier to recognise when preceded by *o* (as a dignified form of address, for example in prayers to gods), though this is usually better omitted in English.

> cenam mihi para, serve.
> Prepare dinner for me, slave!

> adiuvate nos, o deae.
> Help us, goddesses!

• For the *locative*, which has no connection with the vocative but is another (and much rarer) case additional to those usually listed, see page 43.

Accusative case

The accusative gets its name from *accuso* (= I accuse). That may not seem very informative, but it captures by one example the idea of *homing in on a target*: this is what the accusative does, in two main ways.

(1) It is used for the *direct object*, the person or thing on the receiving end of the action expressed by the verb:

> puer librum incendit.
> The boy burned the book.

(2) It is used, with or without a preposition (see below and page 41), to express *motion towards* (the destination being thought of as a target just as the direct object is):

> Romam profecti sumus.
> We set out for Rome.

Regular accusative endings for the three main declensions:

	first	*second*	*third*
sg	-am	-um	-em *(like nom if n)*
pl	-as	-os (-a *if n*)	-es (-a *if n*)

Note that the verbs *doceo* (= I teach) and *rogo* (= I ask) can take a double accusative:

> dominus servum nova verba docuit.
> The master taught the slave some new words.

This must be distinguished from a hidden indirect object, where one of the nouns is actually dative (see page 6):

> senex pecuniam servo dedit.
> The old man gave the slave the money (*i.e.* gave it *to* him).

The accusative is used with prepositions expressing *motion towards* or *through* (see page 41):

> ad Italiam navigavimus.
> We sailed towards Italy.

With the names of towns (and islands small enough to count as one town) the preposition is omitted.

The idea of *motion through* also explains why the accusative is used for *time how long* (see page 75):

> multas horas in villa manebamus.
> We stayed in the house for many hours.

The accusative is used as *subject* of the infinitive in an indirect statement (see page 92):

> nuntius dixit turbam convenire.
> The messenger said that a crowd was gathering.

For the way to deal with a sentence whose first word is accusative, see page 1.

Genitive case

The genitive gets its name from the adjective form of the Latin *genitus*, meaning *birth* or *origin* (compare *Genesis*). The underlying idea is the *source* from which something comes, but in practice the genitive normally expresses *possession* (things *belonging to* people being imagined as *originating from* them). It is translated *of*, or (often more naturally) represented by the use of an apostrophe (before *s* for a singular, after it for a plural):

> haec est senatoris villa.
> This is the house of the senator.
> *or* This is the senator's house.

Regular genitive endings for the three main declensions:

	first	*second*	*third*
sg	-ae	-i	-is
pl	-arum	-orum	-(i)um

As well as expressing possession, the genitive is used in many other places where English uses *of*. A genitive plural often follows a superlative (see page 20):

> optimus servorum adest.
> The best (one) of the slaves is here.

More generally, it often expresses *part* of a larger group:

> quattuor librorum legi.
> I have read four of the books.

The word *plus* (= more) is treated as a noun meaning *a larger quantity*, and is always followed by a genitive:

> da mihi plus cibi.
> *literally* Give me more of food!
> *i.e.* Give me more food!

It is also possible to use *multum* (= much) and *nihil* (= nothing) with a genitive in a similar way:

> multum sanguinis vidimus.
> We saw much blood (*literally* much of blood).

> nihil gaudii accipio ubi talia audio.
> I get no pleasure (*literally* nothing of pleasure) when I hear such things.

Note that in these singular examples, the word *of* is omitted when translating the genitive.

• From the additional vocabulary note that the deponent verb *obliviscor* (= I forget, *literally* I am forgetful *of*) is followed by a genitive.

Dative case

The dative case gets its name from *do* (= I give), perfect passive participle *datus*. Its basic idea is of *giving*: literally handing over something to someone, or doing something for them. It is usually translated *to* or *for*.

Regular dative endings for the three main declensions:

	first	*second*	*third*
sg	-ae	-o	-i
pl	-is	-is	-ibus

The dative is used for the *indirect object* of a sentence:

> cives senatori praemium dederunt.
> The citizens gave the senator a prize.

> puella cenam seni paravit.
> The girl prepared dinner for the old man.

In English, if the indirect object comes before the direct, *to* is often omitted (but if the indirect object comes second, *to* must be included):

> femina filio librum dedit.
> The woman gave her son a book.
> *or* The woman gave a book to her son.

Some verbs, because of their meaning, are always followed by a dative instead of an accusative:

credo	I believe, I trust	(I give trust *to* someone)
persuadeo	I persuade	(I apply persuasion *to* someone)
placet	it pleases	(it is pleasing *to* someone)
resisto	I resist	(I put up resistance *to* someone)

• Note similarly from the additional vocabulary:

faveo	I favour	(I give favour *to* someone)
noceo	I harm	(I do harm *to* someone)
parco	I spare	(I show mercy *to* someone)
pareo	I obey	(I give obedience *to* someone)
permitto	I permit	(I give permission *to* someone)

The adjective *similis* (= similar *to*) is followed by a dative for the same reason.

The dative is used for the agent with a gerundive (see page 90):

> nobis festinandum est.
> *literally* There is for us an act of hurrying needing to be done.
> *i.e.* We must hurry.

Ablative case

The ablative gets its name from *ablatus*, the perfect passive participle of *aufero* (= I carry away): so *carried away*. As with the name of the accusative, this does not seem very informative, but it captures one important idea the ablative expresses: *separation* or going away. The ablative is a bit of a ragbag, but many of its meanings are covered by the translations *by*, *with* or *from*.

Regular ablative endings for the three main declensions:

	first	*second*	*third*
sg	-a	-o	-e (*often -i for adjectives*)
pl	-is	-is	-ibus

The ablative is used with prepositions meaning *going away from*, and also (less predictably) ones meaning *staying* in a place (see page 42):

> omnes cives e foro festinaverunt.
> All the citizens hurried out of the forum.

> nemo in foro manebat.
> No-one stayed in the forum.

With a passive verb the ablative is used both for the agent (the person by whom the action is done), with the preposition *a* (*ab* in front of a vowel or *h*), and for the instrument (the thing with which it is done), without a preposition (see page 66 for both):

> rex ab uxore gladio necatus est.
> The king was killed by his wife with a sword.

The ablative is used to express *time when*, and also *time within which* (see page 75):

> amici nostri prima luce profecti paucis horis advenient.
> Our friends, having set out at first light, will be here within a few hours.

A participle phrase not connected grammatically to the rest of the sentence is put in the ablative as an *ablative absolute* (see pages 87-9):

> signo dato, milites urbem oppugnare coeperunt.
> When the signal had been given, the soldiers began to attack the city.

The ablative can be used after a comparative, instead of an expression with *quam*, to mean *than* (see page 19):

> hic puer fratre stultior est.
> This boy is more stupid than his brother.

• From the additional vocabulary note that the deponent verb *utor* (= I use) is followed by an ablative (again ablative as *instrument*).

Exercise 1   Case usage

1   senex pecuniam nobis dedit.
2   pater puellae in illa urbe habitat.
3   omnes Romam festinavimus.
4   frater meus miles est.
5   dominus servis cenam praebuit.
6   milites clamoribus feminarum vocati sunt.
7   hostes Romanorum in castra subito ingressi sunt.
8   cives verbis regis non credebant.
9   dux militum epistulam uxori misit.
10   aperi mihi hanc ianuam, serve!

Declension and gender

A declension is a *type* of noun (or adjective or pronoun), one of several fixed patterns according to which these words change their endings (for different cases, and for singular and plural). We do not have anything very close to this in English: only pronouns change case (for example *I* into *me*: see page 25), but note the different ways English nouns form their plurals:

> most add -*s* (*book* and *books*) or -*es* (*bus* and *buses*)
> a few add a different ending (*child* and *children*)
> a few change a vowel (*man* and *men*)
> a few stay the same (*sheep*)

Latin declensions are roughly comparable to this. In English the unusual plurals are just minor exceptions to one general rule, but in Latin there are three main patterns (plus two much less common ones).

Gender is the sex which a word has or is imagined to have. In French everything is either masculine or feminine. In English most inanimate objects are regarded as neuter (*it*), though for example a ship is thought of as feminine (... *all who sail in* her). Latin has a neuter gender, but still regards most objects as masculine or feminine.

Declension is not the same as gender, but there is some correlation between them. The vast majority of first declension nouns are feminine, but a few are masculine. Second declension nouns ending -*us* are the other way round: almost all are masculine. There are variant versions of the second and of the third declension for nouns which are neuter: with neuter nouns the accusative is always the same as the nominative, and the nominative and accusative plural always end in -*a*.

A few nouns, e.g. *civis* (= citizen), can be either masculine or feminine according to context.

First declension nouns

Pattern of endings:

sg	nom	-a
	acc	-am
	gen	-ae
	dat	-ae
	abl	-a
pl	nom	-ae
	acc	-as
	gen	-arum
	dat	-is
	abl	-is

		girl *f*
sg	nom	puell-a
	acc	puell-am
	gen	puell-ae
	dat	puell-ae
	abl	puell-a
pl	nom	puell-ae
	acc	puell-as
	gen	puell-arum
	dat	puell-is
	abl	puell-is

Most first declension nouns are feminine, but a few are masculine, for example *nauta* (= sailor).

Most of the other exceptions, not included in GCSE, also refer to male jobs or roles: there is no obvious reason for this. See page 8 on declension and gender. An adjective or participle referring to a masculine first declension noun must be masculine (*nauta bonus* = a good sailor): see page 18 on agreement of nouns and adjectives.

There is no neuter version of the first declension.

The nominative and ablative singular both end in -*a*, but they differ in pronunciation. In the nominative the *a* is short, as in *bat*; in the ablative it is long, as in *father*.

Note also that the genitive and dative singular and the nominative plural endings are all the same (-*ae*). Ambiguous forms have to be worked out from the context.

Second declension nouns

Pattern of endings:

sg	nom	-us*	(-um *if n, with no separate voc*)
	acc	-um	
	gen	-i	
	dat	-o	
	abl	-o	
	(*voc	-e)	
pl	nom	-i	(-a *if n*)
	acc	-os	(-a *if n*)
	gen	-orum	
	dat	-is	
	abl	-is	

		master *m*	war *n*
sg	nom	domin-us*	bell-um
	acc	domin-um	bell-um
	gen	domin-i	bell-i
	dat	domin-o	bell-o
	abl	domin-o	bell-o
	(*voc	domin-e: see page 3)	
pl	nom	domin-i	bell-a
	acc	domin-os	bell-a
	gen	domin-orum	bell-orum
	dat	domin-is	bell-is
	abl	domin-is	bell-is

Nouns like *dominus* are nearly all masculine, but *humus* (= ground) is feminine.

Note that with nouns like *dominus* the genitive singular is the same as the nominative plural, and that with all second declension nouns the dative is like the ablative, both in the singular and in the plural. With neuter nouns like *bellum* the nominative is like the accusative. Ambiguous forms have to be worked out from the context.

Note that *locus* (= place) is masculine in the singular, but has a neuter plural *loca*.

Second declension masculine nouns with nominative singular ending in *-r* behave as if *-us* had disappeared:

		man *m*	boy *n*
sg	*nom*	vir	puer
	acc	vir-um	puer-um
	gen	vir-i	puer-i
		etc	*etc*

As a further slight variant, the following is similar to *puer*, but loses the *-e-* from the stem after the nominative (reflecting the fact that it would be dropped in pronunciation):

		book *m*
sg	*nom*	liber
	acc	libr-um
	gen	libr-i
		etc

Note the following special expressions involving first and second declension nouns:

> poenas do   I pay the penalty (*literally* give penalties), I am punished
> bellum gero   I wage war

• Note that the sense of the verb *gero* varies according to context: it also means *wear* clothes.

• Note from the additional vocabulary that *magister* (= master, schoolmaster, foreman) declines like *liber*.

Exercise 2   First and second declension nouns

1   nauta villam in insula aedificavit.
2   pueri dona in templum deae portabant.
3   muros tabernae celeriter delevimus.
4   femina epistulam mariti non intellexit.
5   Romani multos annos bellum gerebant.
6   lacrimae ancillae domino tandem persuaserunt.
7   filius liberti cibum postulavit.
8   multi libri de vita reginae scripti sunt.
9   servus scelestus poenas dare debet.
10   turba virorum in foro adest.

Third declension nouns

This is slightly more difficult as the nominative singular can end in many different ways, but the endings for the other cases (added to the *stem*, as explained below) again follow a definite pattern.

Pattern of endings:

sg	nom	(wide range of possibilities)	
	acc	-em	(*same as nom if n*)
	gen	-is	
	dat	-i	
	abl	-e	
pl	nom	-es	(-a *if n*)
	acc	-es	(-a *if n*)
	gen	-(i)um	
	dat	-ibus	
	abl	-ibus	

		king	shout	ship	name
		m	*m*	*f*	*n*
sg	nom	rex	clamor	nav-is	nomen
	acc	reg-em	clamor-em	nav-em	nomen
	gen	reg-is	clamor-is	nav-is	nomin-is
	dat	reg-i	clamor-i	nav-i	nomin-i
	abl	reg-e	clamor-e	nav-e	nomin-e
pl	nom	reg-es	clamor-es	nav-es	nomin-a
	acc	reg-es	clamor-es	nav-es	nomin-a
	gen	reg-um	clamor-um	nav-ium	nomin-um
	dat	reg-ibus	clamor-ibus	nav-ibus	nomin-ibus
	abl	reg-ibus	clamor-ibus	nav-ibus	nomin-ibus

For masculine and feminine words, form and gender are not necessarily connected: many feminine nouns follow a pattern similar to *rex*, and many masculine ones decline like *navis*.

With first and second declension nouns (see pages 9-11), the nominative singular always shows what the stem is (for example *dominus*, stem *domin-*). This works for some third declension nouns (for example *clamor*, where the nominative simply is the stem, or *navis*, where the ending -*is* can easily be removed to show the stem *nav-*), but often the nominative is changed a bit, so that the stem is concealed (for example *rex*, concealing the stem *reg-*).

As well as the nominative therefore you always need to know the stem of a third declension noun, in order to work out the other bits. (This is less of a problem than it may seem: nouns within the third declension fall into sub-groups, and when you have seen a few you can often predict the stem. Also, English derivatives often give a clue to the stem: thus *military* from *miles*, stem *milit-*).

Nouns of all declensions are usually quoted in lists and dictionaries with the nominative and genitive singular (see the vocabulary in the back of this book: pages 133-47). This is particularly important for third declension nouns, where the genitive shows the stem. We use the genitive for this purpose because quoting the accusative would be fine for masculine and feminine nouns, but would not work for neuter ones, where the stem is not used until we get to the genitive. So for example:

> custos, custodis *m*   guard

The genitive *custodis* shows that the stem is *custod-*. Often an abbreviated form is used to save space, not repeating the syllable or syllables that stay the same:

> custos, -odis *(for* custodis*) m*   guard
> legio, -onis   *(for* legionis*) f*   legion

Nominative, stem, and gender give all the information needed to work out any bit of a regular noun.

• Note that the genitive plural in the third declension is sometimes *-um*, sometimes *-ium*. A rule which explains most examples of this distinction says that the genitive plural should be one syllable longer than the nominative singular: if the genitive singular is already one syllable longer (as with *rex* or *clamor*), there is no need to increase it again for the genitive plural (so it is *-um*), but if there is no increase in the singular (as with *navis*), there has to be in the plural (so it is *-ium*). But there are exceptions. Many words whose nominative singular is a single syllable, for example *urbs* (= city) increase twice: *urbs, urbis, urbium* (though *rex* does not).

All nominative and accusative plurals in the third declension (and as usual also nominative and accusative neuter singulars) are *ambiguous* forms: you cannot tell in isolation which case they are, but context and word order normally enable you to work it out. So for example:

> cives nuntios laudant.
> The citizens praise the messengers.

Here the second declension *nuntios* is accusative, so *cives* must be nominative.

> nuntii cives laudant.
> The messengers praise the citizens.

Here the second declension *nuntii* is nominative, so *cives* must be accusative.

13

• There are also possibilities for confusion with endings of other declensions. The third declension genitive plural ending in *-um* or *-ium* might be mistaken for a second declension accusative singular such as *dominum* or *filium*. The third declension nominative or genitive singular *-is* might be mistaken for the dative or ablative plural of a first or second declension noun (though those endings have a long *i* and so are pronounced differently). As with any neuter plural ending in *-a*, there is the risk of confusion with a first declension noun like *puella* (but if the neuter plural is nominative it will of course have a plural verb). Thorough learning of both vocabulary and declensions is the safest way to avoid such problems, but intelligent deduction from sense and context will also take you a long way.

• Note that the following third declension nouns are usually masculine, but can be also be feminine, according to the sex of the people described (by convention a mixed group is regarded as masculine):

masculine):	civis, -is	citizen
	comes, -itis	companion
	custos, -odis	guard

• From the extra vocabulary, note the irregular/defective noun *vis* (*f*) = force (acc *vim*, abl *vi*; no other parts of the singular exist); pl *vires* = strength, military forces (gen *virium*). Care needs to be taken to avoid confusing this with *vir* (= man).

Exercise 3   Third declension nouns

1   milites vocem imperatoris audire non poterant.
2   nonne nomen custodis cognovisti?
3   multae naves ab hostibus delebantur.
4   frater senatoris fortissimus erat.
5   eo tempore duo legiones ibi pugnabant.
6   iter difficile per montes ad mare facere debebimus.
7   pater regis a custodibus servatus est.
8   uxor militis vulnera eius per totam noctem curabat.
9   corpus senis sanguine celatum est.
10   princeps matrem meam laudavit.

Exercise 4   First, second and third declension nouns (revision)

1   liberti in taberna diu laborabant.
2   senex uxorem bene curabat.
3   comites nostrae in horto humi iacent.
4   naves regis trans omnia maria navigant.
5   domina mea epistulam filio misit.
6   cives periculum belli diu timebant.
7   per silvam ad flumen ambulabam.
8   consiliumne novum habet dux noster?
9   servus ianuam villae mihi aperuit.
10   cur templum deae non intravisti?

Fourth and fifth declension nouns

These are much less common than the first three declensions. There are only a few of each, but they include some important words. Fourth declension can be thought of as a variant of second, and fifth as a variant of third.

		FOURTH DECLENSION	FIFTH DECLENSION
		hand, *or* group of people	day
		f	*m (or f)*
sg	*nom*	man-us	di-es
	acc	man-um	di-em
	gen	man-us	di-ei
	dat	man-ui	di-ei
	abl	man-u	di-e
pl	*nom*	man-us	di-es
	acc	man-us	di-es
	gen	man-uum	di-erum
	dat	man-ibus	di-ebus
	abl	man-ibus	di-ebus

• The two different meanings of *manus* are linked by the idea of a group of people as a *handful*.

• There are both masculine and feminine nouns in both the fourth and the fifth declension (there is also a neuter version of fourth, but there are no examples in the GCSE vocabulary).

• Four different bits of a word like *manus* (nominative and genitive singular, nominative and accusative plural) are spelled in the same way (the *u* in the nominative singular is pronounced short, the others long). The number and case have to be worked out from the context. Note in particular that if the word is accusative, it must also be plural:

> hic servus magnas manus habet.
> This slave has big hands.

• Note that *domus* (= house) has the ablative singular *domo* (and usually the accusative plural *domos*) as if it were second declension: see page 10, and page 43 for its locative *domi*.

• Note that *dies* is usually masculine, but in the singular can be feminine if it refers to a special day.

• Note that *res* has a range of meanings: *thing*, *business*, but also *story* (*totam rem narravit* = he told the whole story).

Exercise 5   Fourth and fifth declension nouns

1   nullam spem pacis habemus.
2   frater meus paucis diebus adveniet.
3   nuntius vultu misero totam rem regi narravit.
4   cuius manu scripta est haec epistula?
5   manum militum prope domum manentem conspeximus.

Adjectives

There are two basic types: one which is a mixture of first and second declensions (second in the masculine and neuter, first in the feminine), and another which is third declension (with masculine and feminine the same, and a variant form for the neuter).

FIRST AND SECOND DECLENSION (2-1-2)

good

		m	f	n
sg	nom	bon-us	bon-a	bon-um
	acc	bon-um	bon-am	bon-um
	gen	bon-i	bon-ae	bon-i
	dat	bon-o	bon-ae	bon-o
	abl	bon-o	bon-a	bon-o
pl	nom	bon-i	bon-ae	bon-a
	acc	bon-os	bon-as	bon-a
	gen	bon-orum	bon-arum	bon-orum
	dat	bon-is	bon-is	bon-is
	abl	bon-is	bon-is	bon-is

This is exactly like the three nouns *dominus, puella, bellum* (see pages 9 and 10). Nouns are usually dealt with in declension order (first, second) but for adjectives the convention is to set them out in gender order: masculine, feminine, neuter.

• A similar layout is used for pronouns (pages 25-40) and participles (pages 80-6).

This set of forms is very important: it is used in many different contexts and will be referred to constantly. Understanding it thoroughly means a big reduction in mechanical learning. It is described in this book as *2-1-2*. This is shorthand for *2m-1f-2n*: second declension masculine like *dominus*, first declension feminine like *puella*, second declension neuter like *bellum* (there is no need to quote the genders each time because the order is always *m, f, n*).

Note that for the masculine and feminine forms here, gender and declension are in effect equated: each gender uses the endings of the declension where most of the nouns belong to that gender (see page 8 on gender and declension).

There are a few adjectives with masculine nominative singular ending *-er* (compare the nouns on page 11):

> *miser* (= miserable) keeps the *e* like *puer* does, hence accusative *miserum*;
> *pulcher* (= beautiful) drops the *e* like *liber* does, hence accusative *pulchrum*.

For the third declension type, it is useful to study two models (others can be worked out):

THIRD DECLENSION

brave, strong

		m/f	*n*
sg	*nom*	fort-is	fort-e
	acc	fort-em	fort-e
	gen	fort-is	fort-is
	dat	fort-i	fort-i
	abl	fort-i	fort-i
pl	*nom*	fort-es	fort-ia
	acc	fort-es	fort-ia
	gen	fort-ium	fort-ium
	dat	fort-ibus	fort-ibus
	abl	fort-ibus	fort-ibus

The masculine/feminine version of this is almost identical to the noun *navis* (see page 12), but note that *fortis*, like most third declension adjectives, has *-i* (instead of the *-e* which the nouns have) in the ablative singular. The form *forte* is used instead for the neuter. As usual with neuter words, the nominative and accusative (in both singular and plural) are the same as each other, and the nominative and accusative plural end in *-a* (here *-ia*: compare how the genitive plural is *-ium* rather than *-um*, and see page 13).

• Note that *celer* (= swift) is third declension and behaves as if it had started *celeris* (and in fact does so in the feminine, which here unusually differs from the masculine).

THIRD DECLENSION

huge

		m/f	*n*
sg	*nom*	ingens	ingens
	acc	ingent-em	ingens
	gen	ingent-is	ingent-is
	dat	ingent-i	ingent-i
	abl	ingent-i	ingent-i
pl	*nom*	ingent-es	ingent-ia
	acc	ingent-es	ingent-ia
	gen	ingent-ium	ingent-ium
	dat	ingent-ibus	ingent-ibus
	abl	ingent-ibus	ingent-ibus

Agreement of nouns and adjectives

Every adjective must *agree* with the noun it refers to in number, gender and case. If a noun is first or second declension *and* the adjective is of 2-1-2 form, the endings will often actually be identical: for example *amicos bonos* = good friends (accusative plural). This will often be true as well if the noun is third declension *and* the adjective also is: for example *militem fortem* = a brave soldier (accusative singular). But exact matching of forms (or 'rhyming') like this is a bonus: it is NOT what *agreeing* means. The adjective must follow the gender of the noun, and it must be in the right number and case. Sometimes that will produce an identical ending, sometimes not.

Adjectives normally come after the noun they refer to. But a few common ones (most of them referring to size or quantity) usually come in front, like English adjectives do:

magnus -a -um	big
parvus -a -um	small
multus -a -um	much, *pl* many
pauci -ae -a	few
omnis -e	all
novus -a -um	new

Note also that any adjective can be used on its own *as* a noun: in such cases a suitable noun has to be *supplied* in English from the grammar and context:

nuntius multa dixit.
The messenger said many *things*.

dea bonos adiuvat.
The goddess helps good *men/people* (*or* the good, *as a category*).

Here there is no separate words for *things* or *men/people*: they have to be worked out and supplied from the fact that *multa* is neuter, *bonos* is masculine, and both plural.

• Note that the adjectives *medius -a -um* (= middle) and *summus -a -um* (= highest, top) are often used to mean *middle/top of*, i.e. *summus mons* usually means *the top of the mountain*, rather than *the highest mountain* (of several).

• Note from the additional vocabulary that the neuter plural *bona* is used as a noun meaning *goods* (= property), like the equivalent English.

Exercise 6   Agreement of nouns and adjectives

1   nauta Romanus a servo audaci necatus est.
2   senex bonus librum brevem scripsit.
3   rex pessimus multa dira fecit.
4   cives stulti equum infelicem in urbem duxerunt.
5   clamor ingens ab omnibus pueris audiebatur.

Comparative adjectives

A *comparative* adjective is used to compare two people or things, to express the fact that one has a particular quality to a greater extent than another. In English a comparative is usually formed by adding *-er* to a short word (*long* becomes *longer*), or putting *more* in front of a longer word (*complicated* becomes *more complicated*).

		longer *m/f*	*n*
sg	*nom*	longior	longius
	acc	longior-em	longius
	gen	longior-is	longior-is
	dat	longior-i	longior-i
	abl	longior-e	longior-e
pl	*nom*	longior-es	longior-a
	acc	longior-es	longior-a
	gen	longior-um	longior-um
	dat	longior-ibus	longior-ibus
	abl	longior-ibus	longior-ibus

The syllable *-ior* is added to the basic stem, and the comparative form is third declension (see pages 12 and 17). This applies regardless of whether the ordinary adjective is 2-1-2 (as *longus* is) or third declension (like for example *fortis*). Note that the ablative here is *-e*, like the nouns (see page 17). Irregular comparatives (see page 21) use these same endings.

• Note the distinctive neuter form (which might be mistaken for a second declension masculine form like *filius*): this is also used for the comparative *adverb* (see page 24).

A comparative adjective is very often followed by *quam* (= than). The two people or things being compared will be in the same case. In a simple comparison this is often nominative:

> dominus stultior est quam servus.
> The master is more stupid than the slave (is).

But they can be in any case, according to their job in the sentence:

> senex librum multo longiorem mihi quam fratri dedit.
> The old man gave a much longer book to me than (he gave) to my brother.

• The adverb *multo* (= much) is often used with a comparative to stress the amount of difference.

A simple comparison can alternatively be expressed by missing out *quam* and putting the second noun in the ablative (*ablative of comparison*):

> dominus stultior est servo.
> *literally* The master is more stupid, by (the side of *or* the standard of) the slave.
> *i.e.* The master is more stupid than the slave.

Superlative adjectives

A *superlative* adjective tells us that a person or thing has a quality to a very great extent, or to the greatest extent of any in a group. In English the first meaning is expressed by using *very*, the second usually by adding *-est* to a short word (*long* becomes *longest*), or putting *most* in front of a long word (*complicated* becomes *most complicated*).

		longest, very long		
		m	*f*	*n*
sg	*nom*	longissim-us	longissim-a	longissim-um
	acc	longissim-um	longissim-am	longissim-um
		etc	*etc*	*etc*

The syllables *-issim-* are added to the basic stem, and the superlative is regular 2-1-2 in form (see page 16). This applies regardless of whether the ordinary adjective is 2-1-2 (as *longus* is) or third declension (like for example *fortis*). Irregular superlatives (see page 21) use these same endings.

The context usually enables you to tell whether *very* or *-est/most* is the appropriate translation.

> quod epistulam tuam acceperat, puella laetissima erat.
> Because she had received your letter, the girl was very happy.

> hic servus stultissimus omnium est.
> This slave is the most stupid of all (the slaves).

The use of a genitive plural after a superlative, as in the second example, is a reliable indication that *the most ...* is needed in English.

Exercise 7   Comparative and superlative adjectives (regular)

1   librum difficiliorem numquam legi.
2   miles ferocissimus puerum terruit.
3   hic servus fidelior est quam ceteri.
4   mare illo die saevissimum erat.
5   libertus nunc laetior est quam dominus a quo liberatus est.
6   haec via brevissima est.
7   ille senex filio fortior est.
8   milites Romani audacissimi sunt.
9   hic puer stultior est fratre.
10   montem altissimum in insula conspeximus.

Irregular comparative and superlative adjectives

An adjective is often shown with its comparative and superlative forms:

ordinary form		*comparative*	*superlative*
longus	*long*	longior	longissimus

This is particularly useful if they are irregular. A number of adjectives have slightly irregular superlatives which are still very easy to recognise.

• 2-1-2 adjectives with masculine nominative singular ending *-er* (and the third declension *celer*) have the superlative ending *-errimus* :

miser	*miserable*	miserior	miserrimus
pulcher	*beautiful*	pulchrior	pulcherrimus
celer	*swift*	celerior	celerrimus

• Some third declension adjectives with masculine/feminine nominative singular ending *-ilis* have the superlative ending *-illimus*:

facilis	*easy*	facilior	facillimus
difficilis	*difficult*	difficilior	difficillimus
similis	*similar*	similior	simillimus

More care needs to be taken with the very irregular forms. Note that these are often irregular in English too. In language generally, the most common words are typically the most irregular, because they have got bashed around with use. They quickly become familiar because they are met so often.

bonus	*good*	melior	*better*	optimus	*best*
malus	*bad*	peior	*worse*	pessimus	*worst*
magnus	*big*	maior	*bigger*	maximus	*biggest*
parvus	*small*	minor	*smaller*	minimus	*smallest*
multus	*much*	plus	*more (of)*	plurimus	*most (of)*
multi	*many*	plures	*more*	plurimi	*most*

• Note that *plus* in the singular behaves like a neuter noun meaning *a greater amount*, for example *plus cibi* (= more food): see page 5.

Exercise 8   Comparative and superlative adjectives (irregular)

1   plurimi nautae in foro aderant.
2   senator quidam domum maximam aedificavit.
3   puellam pulcherrimam heri vidi.
4   pater plus pecuniae mihi quam fratri meo dedit.
5   consilium tuum melius meo est.
6   plures milites in silva quam in castris manebant.
7   lux iter facillimum fecit.
8   peiorem servum numquam vidi.
9   rex terram minimam habebat.
10   librum optimum nunc habeo.

Adverbs

Adverbs usually describe verbs, just as adjectives describe nouns (adverbs can also describe adjectives, or other adverbs).

(1) Many adverbs have a corresponding adjective, from which they are formed.

We had a slow journey.   *adjective*
We travelled slowly.   *adverb*

As this example illustrates, adverbs formed from adjectives in English often end *-ly* (though we cannot for example say *difficultly*, but have to use a more roundabout expression: *with difficulty* or *in a difficult way*).

For 2-1-2 adjectives (see page 16) the adverb is formed by removing *-us* from the masculine nominative singular and adding -e to the stem. So for example:

laetus   happy   *adjective*
laete   happily   *adverb*

• Note that the adverb from *bonus* (= good) is *bene* (= well).

For third declension adjectives (see page 17) the adverb is formed by adding *-iter* to the stem. So for example:

brevis   brief   *adjective*
breviter   briefly   *adverb*

• Sometimes the *i* in the ending is dropped and just *-ter* is added to the stem: *audax* (= bold), stem *audac-*, adverb *audacter*. If the stem already ends in *t* just *-er* is added.

• Although *facilis* (= easy) and *difficilis* (= difficult) are third declension, they form their adverbs by adding *-e*: hence *facile*, *difficile*.

• Note that the adverb from *fortis* (= brave *or* strong) is *fortiter*. The adverb *forte* (= by chance) is unconnected: it comes from the same root as *fortune* in English. Confusion of these two words is a very common mistake in GCSE: see page 115. (The form *forte* could be the neuter nominative or accusative of *fortis*, but this is much less likely to be met than the adverb *by chance*.)

Exercise 9   Adverbs (from adjectives)

1   puella donum laete accepit.
2   senex breviter respondit.
3   dominus servis severe locutus est.
4   nonne tu pecuniam fideliter custodire potes?
5   omnes fortiter pugnaverunt.   (continued ...)

6	quis illa verba stulte scripsit?
7	dominus e villa irate discessit.
8	puer pecuniam senis audacter et crudeliter rapuit.
9	rex civibus omnia haec vere promisit.
10	hostes urbem nostram saeve oppugnaverunt.

(2) There are many other adverbs, not formed from adjectives, which indicate (for example) *when*, *why* or *how* something happens:

antea	before, previously	nunc	now
deinde	then, next	olim	once, some time ago
diu	for a long time	paene	almost
forte	by chance	postea	afterwards
frustra	in vain	postridie	on the next day
heri	yesterday	saepe	often
hic	here	satis	enough
hodie	today	semper	always
iam	now, already	sic	thus, in this way
ibi	there	statim	at once, immediately
ita	in this way	subito	suddenly
iterum	again	tandem	at last
mox	soon	tum	then
numquam	never		

• Other adverbs are explained with the construction of which they form part: question words (for example *cur* = why?) with direct questions (page 73), signpost words (for example *tam* = so) with result clauses (page 102).

Exercise 10   Adverbs (not formed from adjectives)

1	nuntius media nocte forte advenit.
2	nihil postea audivimus.
3	omnia iam parata sunt.
4	pecunia diu quaerebatur.
5	de his rebus satis scio.
6	haec navis iam plena est.
7	illum librum saepe lego.
8	frater meus mox adveniet.
9	Romam frustra festinavimus.
10	hostes urbem iterum oppugnaverunt.

Comparative and superlative adverbs

The comparative form of an adverb formed from an adjective is the *neuter singular* of the comparative adjective (nominative/accusative form): the distinctive but misleading ending *-ius* (see page 19). Hence for example:

comparative   laetius   more happily

Because a superlative adjective is 2-1-2 in declension (see page 16), the adverb form of it is predictably formed in the same way as the adverb of a normal 2-1-2 adjective: remove *-us* from the masculine nominative singular and add *-e* (see page 22). So for example:

superlative   laetissime   very happily, most happily

These rules apply to irregular as well as regular comparatives and superlatives.

A comparative adverb is often followed by *quam* (= than), just as a comparative adjective is (see page 19):

> senator civibus facilius persuasit quam ego.
> The senator persuaded the citizens more easily than I (did).

Note a different meaning of *quam* when it is attached to a superlative adverb:

> quam celerrime   as quickly as possible

Some adverbs not formed from adjectives (see page 23) have a comparative and superlative following the same pattern. Note in particular:

	diu	for a long time	saepe	often
comparative	diutius	for a longer time	saepius	more often
superlative	diutissime	for a very long time	saepissime	very/most often

Exercise 11   Comparative and superlative adverbs

1	femina epistulam difficilem optime scripsit.
2	ancilla nova melius loquitur quam omnes aliae.
3	pueri cenam quam celerrime consumpserunt.
4	talia nunc saepius accidunt quam antea.
5	cives nuntium laetissime acceperunt.
6	rex homini scelesto iratissime respondit.
7	nemo fortius pugnavit quam dux noster.
8	iuvenes Romani maxime gaudebant.
9	ego celeriter cucurri, sed servus celerius effugit.
10	muri a militibus fortissime custodiebantur.

Pronouns

A pronoun is a word such as *I*, *she*, *they* which stands in place of a noun and avoids the need to repeat it.

Some of the common pronouns in English are the only words which have case endings like Latin:

I (*nominative*) changes to	me (*accusative*)
he	him
she	her
they	them
who	whom (*though this is falling out of use*)

Nominative pronouns are omitted in Latin if the subject of a sentence can be worked out from the verb ending.

Words such as *this* and *that* are classed as pronouns, though when used with a noun they become adjectives. *Possessives*, words indicating the person something belongs to (*my*, *your*), are also included here, though they are normally used as adjectives.

Latin has a lot of pronouns. Confusion over some of the less common ones is a very common mistake in GCSE. On the other hand pronouns are formed according to fixed patterns (explained below), cutting down the amount of learning needed.

Summary of pronouns for basic recognition:

ego (*acc* me)	I (me)
nos	we
tu	you (*sg*)
vos	you (*pl*)
is, ea, id	he, she, it
se	him/her/itself
hic	this
ille	that
ipse	self
idem	the same
qui	who
quis	who?
quidam	a certain
aliquis	someone
alter	one of two
ceteri	the rest
nemo	no-one

Personal pronouns

FIRST PERSON

I, me, *pl* we, us

sg	*nom*	ego
	acc	me
	gen	mei
	dat	mihi
	abl	me
pl	*nom*	nos
	acc	nos
	gen	nostrum
	dat	nobis
	abl	nobis

SECOND PERSON

you (*sg and pl*)

sg	*nom*	tu
	acc	te
	gen	tui
	dat	tibi
	abl	te
pl	*nom*	vos
	acc	vos
	gen	vestrum
	dat	vobis
	abl	vobis

First and second person pronouns in the nominative are normally used only for emphasis or to draw a contrast, as the subject can be worked out from the verb ending:

> nos semper laboramus.
> *We* are always working (*implying* but others are not).

> ego dicam, et tu audies.
> I shall speak, and you will listen.

In the other cases they can be used in a reflexive sense (referring back to a first or second person subject):

> gladio me defendo.
> I defend myself with a sword.

26

The accusative is often used in this reflexive way as the subject of an infinitive in indirect statement (see pages 92-6):

> promisi me rediturum esse.
> I promised that I would return.

When these pronouns in the ablative are used with the preposition *cum* (= with), it is stuck on the end (*mecum, tecum, nobiscum, vobiscum*): see below, and page 42.

• For the associated possessive adjectives *meus, noster, tuus, vester* (= my, our, your) see page 29.

THIRD PERSON REFLEXIVE

> himself, herself, itself, *pl* themselves

sg and pl

	(*no nom*)
acc	se
gen	sui
dat	sibi
abl	se

Note that *se* cannot be translated in isolation, but only in its context in a sentence. It always refers back to the subject, and gets its gender and number from there.

> puella sibi cenam paravit.
> The girl prepared dinner for herself.

Like the first and second person pronouns, *se* when used in the ablative with the preposition *cum* (= with) has it stuck on the end:

> imperator matrem secum duxit.
> The emperor took his mother with him.

• For the associated possessive adjective *suus* (= his/her/its/their own) see page 29.

• The reflexive *se* (always third person, and never nominative) must be distinguished carefully from *ipse* (= self) which does not have these restrictions: see page 33.

• For the use of *se* as the subject of an infinitive in indirect statement see page 95.

• With some verbs the reflexive is used in Latin but not translated (English just uses the verb in an intransitive sense):

> puer in templo se celavit.
> The boy hid in the temple.

This applies also to first and second person reflexives.

THIRD PERSON

he, she, it, *pl* they, them (*can also mean* that, those)

		m	f	n
sg	*nom*	is	ea	id
	acc	eum	eam	id
	gen	<u>eius</u>	<u>eius</u>	<u>eius</u>
	dat	<u>ei</u>	<u>ei</u>	<u>ei</u>
	abl	eo	ea	eo
pl	*nom*	ei	eae	ea
	acc	eos	eas	ea
	gen	eorum	earum	eorum
	dat	eis	eis	eis
	abl	eis	eis	eis

Note the distinctive genitive and dative singular endings (*-ius* and *-i*), across all three genders. These are also used for many other pronouns, and are similarly underlined in other tables of pronouns in this book (and the number *one*: see page 74).

Note that the plural is regular 2-1-2 in declension (see page 16).

• This word can also be used like *ille* (see page 31) to mean *that*.

• The adverbs *antea* (= before, previously) and *postea* (= afterwards) are in origin the pronouns *ante* and *post* plus the neuter plural *ea* (see pages 41 and 75).

• For the genitive of this pronoun used as a possessive (*his, hers, its, their*) see page 30.

Exercise 12   Personal pronouns

1   tu miles eris, ego nauta.
2   puellae in silva se celaverunt.
3   ego celerius currere possum quam vos omnes.
4   num pater me hic videbit?
5   liberi cenam sibi parabant.
6   tune librum scripsisti?
7   rex nobis praemium dedit.
8   paucos vestrum antea vidi.
9   nihil tibi offere possumus, sceleste.
10   dea hominibus se olim ostendit.

Possessives

A possessive indicates who something belongs to (e.g. *my, your*). Most of these are straightforward and decline as 2-1-2 adjectives (see page 16).

FIRST PERSON

my

		m	*f*	*n*
sg	*nom*	meus	mea	meum
	acc	meum	meam	meum

our

sg	*nom*	noster	nostra	nostrum
	acc	nostrum	nostram	nostrum

SECOND PERSON

your (belonging to you *sg*)

sg	*nom*	tuus	tua	tuum
	acc	tuum	tuam	tuum

your (belonging to you *pl*)

sg	*nom*	vester	vestra	vestrum
	acc	vestrum	vestram	vestrum

In the third person it is a bit more complicated. There are two different ways of expressing *his/her/its/their*, according to whether or not the possessive refers back to the subject of the sentence. If it does, the adjective *suus* is used:

THIRD PERSON REFLEXIVE

his/her/its/their (own) (*belonging to whoever is the subject of the sentence*)

		m	*f*	*n*
sg	*nom*	suus	sua	suum
	acc	suum	suam	suum
		etc	*etc*	*etc*

(regular 2-1-2: see page 16)

• Note that *suus* cannot be translated out of context. Its meaning depends on who is the subject of the sentence. Its number and gender are those of the thing possessed, not the possessor. Thus it is NOT the case, as you might think, that the masculine means *his*, the feminine *her*, and the plural *their*: any part of *suus* can mean any of these, depending on the number and gender of the subject.

• Note the use of *suos* (masculine plural, without a noun), usually meaning *his men* (i.e. soldiers):

>   imperator suos in periculum duxit.
>   The general led his men into danger.

Alternatively it may refer to a mixed group, and take its meaning from the subject and context (*literally* his/her/their <u>own people</u>):

>   puella capta promisit suos pecuniam missuros esse.
>   The girl who had been captured promised that her family would send money.

When the reference of *his/her/its/their* is to someone other than the subject, there is no adjective and so the genitive of the pronoun *is, ea, id* (see page 28) is used instead: literally *of him, of her, of it*. This time the number and gender ARE those of the possessor, though in the singular all three genders are the same anyway (*eius*).

• Note carefully that the ending of the possessive *eius* is the distinctive *-ius* genitive of a pronoun (see page 28), NOT the masculine nominative singular of a 2-1-2 adjective, as it is with *suus*.

THIRD PERSON NON-REFLEXIVE

his/her/its (*belonging to someone who is not the subject of the sentence*)

	m	*f*	*n*
sg	eius	eius	eius

their (*belonging to people who are not the subject of the sentence*)

	m	*f*	*n*
pl	eorum	earum	eorum

• For the third person non-reflexive possessive, the genitive of a pronoun is used because no adjective is available. Any other possessive could be expressed in this way, but an adjective is used where there is one: *domus mei* (= the house of me) would be intelligible for *my house*, but in practice *domus mea* is used instead.

Exercise 13   Possessives

1	cibus noster semper pessimus est.
2	frater meus libros suos numquam legit.
3	vocem tuam iterum audire nolo.
4	milites duci suo semper credebant.
5	mare nostrum plurimos portus habet.
6	ego hunc senem et uxorem eius heri vidi.
7	frater meus tuum non timet.
8	haec femina et maritum suum et pecuniam eius amat.
9	num urbem vestram odistis, cives?
10	imperator non suum equum sed meum habet.

This and *That*

		m	f	n
		this, pl these		
		m	*f*	*n*
sg	nom	hic	haec	hoc
	acc	hunc	hanc	hoc
	gen	<u>huius</u>	<u>huius</u>	<u>huius</u>
	dat	<u>huic</u>	<u>huic</u>	<u>huic</u>
	abl	hoc	hac	hoc
pl	nom	hi	hae	haec
	acc	hos	has	haec
	gen	horum	harum	horum
	dat	his	his	his
	abl	his	his	his

Again note the distinctive genitive and dative singular endings, the dative here adding -*c* to the -*i* which most pronouns have.

The plural is regular 2-1-2 in declension (see page 16) apart from the neuter nominative and accusative (and even this resembles regular 2-1-2 by being the same as the feminine nominative singular).

		m	f	n
		that, pl those		
		m	*f*	*n*
sg	nom	ille	illa	illud
	acc	illum	illam	illud
	gen	<u>illius</u>	<u>illius</u>	<u>illius</u>
	dat	<u>illi</u>	<u>illi</u>	<u>illi</u>
	abl	illo	illa	illo
pl	nom	illi	illae	illa
	acc	illos	illas	illa
	gen	illorum	illarum	illorum
	dat	illis	illis	illis
	abl	illis	illis	illis

Again note the distinctive genitive and dative singular endings across all three genders.

The plural is regular 2-1-2 in declension (see page 16).

This *and* That

• Note that *this* implies *here*, *near me*, whereas *that* implies *over there*, *further away*.

• Note that the third person pronoun *is*, *ea*, *id* can also be used as an adjective meaning *that* (i.e. the same as *ille*, *illa*, *illud*).

> legistine omnes eos libros?
> Have you read all those books?

The words *this* and *that* illustrate well how pronouns are often used as adjectives. If part of *hic* or *ille* is used with a noun, it usually comes in front of it:

> hic vir nihil nobis dicere potest.　　(hic *as adjective*)
> This man can tell us nothing.

But the same meaning could be expressed by *hic* alone:

> hic nobis nihil dicere potest.　　(hic *as pronoun*)

A word such as *man*, *woman*, *thing*, *people* is supplied in English according to the gender and number of the pronoun.

> iubeo te omnia illa eicere.
> I order you to throw out all those things.

Often *ille* is used for *he* as the subject of a sentence, referring to someone who was mentioned in the previous sentence but was not its subject:

> dominus servum diu petivit. ille tandem rediit.
> The master looked for the slave for a long time. He (*i.e.* the slave) finally returned.

• For the use of the *connecting relative* in a similar way, as the subject of a new sentence, see page 79.

Exercise 14　　*This* and *That*

1　　num omnes has epistulas scripsistis?
2　　dominus huius servi non adest.
3　　clamores illorum civium eam servaverunt.
4　　ille miles semper fortiter pugnat.
5　　hanc solam amo.
6　　ianua illius villae aperta est.
7　　hic equus celerior est illo.
8　　ea verba iterum audire nolo.
9　　illa nocte nihil grave accidit.
10　　nuntius regis haec mihi dixit.

Self and *Same*

		self, *pl* selves		
		m	*f*	*n*
sg	*nom*	ipse	ipsa	ipsum
	acc	ipsum	ipsam	ipsum
	gen	ipsius	ipsius	ipsius
	dat	ipsi	ipsi	ipsi
	abl	ipso	ipsa	ipso
pl	*nom*	ipsi	ipsae	ipsa
	acc	ipsos	ipsas	ipsa
		etc	*etc*	*etc*

(regular 2-1-2 plural: see page 16)

Again note the distinctive genitive and dative singular endings.

Note carefully the distinction between *ipse* and *se* (which is always third person, always reflexive, and never nominative: see page 27). The word *ipse* commonly implies *in person* (not through someone else). Nominative parts of it can be used regardless of person:

> nos ipsi nihil audivimus.
> We ourselves heard nothing.

Though classed as a pronoun, *ipse* is very often used with a noun or another pronoun:

> regem ipsum vidi.
> I saw the king himself.

> illi ipsi omnia audiverunt.
> Those men themselves heard everything.

It can be added to a reflexive (see pages 26-7) for extra emphasis:

> hic miles se ipsum semper laudat.
> This soldier always praises himself.

		the same		
		m	*f*	*n*
sg	*nom*	idem	eadem	idem
	acc	eundem	eandem	idem
	gen	eiusdem	eiusdem	eiusdem
	dat	eidem	eidem	eidem
	abl	eodem	eadem	eodem
pl	*nom*	eidem	eaedem	eadem
	acc	eosdem	easdem	eadem
	gen	eorundem	earundem	eorundem
	dat	eisdem	eisdem	eisdem
	abl	eisdem	eisdem	eisdem

This is the pronoun *is, ea, id* (see page 28) with *-dem* stuck on the end, and minor adjustments of spelling.* Again note the distinctive genitive and dative singular endings (this time with *-dem* added).

* The *-s* of the masculine nominative singular has disappeared, so *idem* not *isdem*. The neuter ending in *-d* already does not double it (so neuter nominative and accusative singular, like masculine nominative, are *idem*). Any part of the original pronoun ending *-m* changes it to *-n* before *-dem* is added, to ease pronunciation (so masculine accusative singular *eundem*, not *eumdem*).

Like other pronouns, parts of *idem* can be used alone (supplying a suitable noun in English from gender, number and context), or as an adjective with a noun:

> hic senex eadem semper dicit.
> This old man always says the same things.

> num eundem librum iterum legere vis?
> Surely you do not want to read the same book again?

Exercise 15   *Self* and *Same*

1   num regis ipsius equum habes?
2   hic puer idem semper rogat.
3   consumpsistisne omnes eundem cibum?
4   multa vera de imperatore ipso dicebantur.
5   haec est villa quam ego ipse aedificavi.
6   nonne templum ipse vidisti?
7   omnes naves eodem modo factae sunt.
8   cives nuntium ipsum de bello rogaverunt.
9   omnes eodem die advenerunt.
10   donum reginae ipsi mittere volo.

Relative pronoun (*who, which*) and clause

		who, which		
		m	*f*	*n*
sg	*nom*	qui	quae	quod
	acc	quem	quam	quod
	gen	cuius	cuius	cuius
	dat	cui	cui	cui
	abl	quo	qua	quo
pl	*nom*	qui	quae	quae
	acc	quos	quas	quae
	gen	quorum	quarum	quorum
	dat	quibus	quibus	quibus
	abl	quibus	quibus	quibus

Note that the plural here is 2-1-2 (see page 16) apart from (a) the neuter nominative and accusative (which however resembles 2-1-2 by being the same as the feminine nominative singular) and (b) the dative and ablative for all three genders, which are *quibus*, not *quis*.

The relative pronoun gets its name from the fact that it *relates* or links two facts about a person or thing:

> servus, quem heri vidi, iterum adest.
> The slave, whom I saw yesterday, is here again.

The relative pronoun refers or *relates back* to a noun which usually comes just before it (and so is called the *antecedent* = preceding). The relative pronoun agrees with the antecedent in *number* and *gender* but NOT necessarily in *case*.

Its case is determined by the job it is doing in its own clause. A relative clause is in effect one sentence stuck inside another. In the example above, the main sentence is:

> servus iterum adest.
> The slave is here again.

The sentence which has been made into the relative clause would on its own be:

> servum heri vidi.
> I saw the slave yesterday.

If we kept it separate but used a pronoun, it would be:

> eum heri vidi.
> I saw him yesterday.

Clearly *him* has to be accusative as it is the object of *vidi*. This is still true when we put this sentence inside the other one as a relative clause.

Note that in English the singular *who* becomes *whom* in the accusative, and *whose* in the genitive. The word *whom* however is dropping out of use, and *who* is commonly used for the accusative too. Alternatively *that* is often used instead (*the slave that I saw*), or the relative pronoun is missed out altogether (*the slave I saw*).

Any combination of cases for antecedent and relative pronoun is possible:

> quaerimus navem quae antea in portu erat.
> We are looking for the ship which was previously in the harbour,

Here the antecedent *navem* is accusative because it is the object of *quaerimus*, and the relative pronoun *quae* is nominative because it is the subject of *erat*.

The relative clause may have both subject and object of its own, with the relative pronoun in another case:

> senex cui puella epistulam misit laetissimus erat.
> The old man to whom the girl sent the letter was very happy.

Here the antecedent *senex* is nominative because it is the subject of *erat*, and the relative pronoun *cui* is dative because if we extracted the clause as a separate sentence, it would be:

> puella seni epistulam misit.
> The girl sent the letter to the old man.

Note that the relative pronoun is often used after parts of the third person pronoun *is, ea, id* (see page 28):

> ei qui fugerant mox capti sunt.
> Those who had run away were soon captured.

• For the use of *qui, quae, quod* as a connecting relative to link sentences together see page 79.

• For the use of *qui, quae, quod* with the subjunctive to express purpose see page 99.

Exercise 16   Relative pronoun and clause

1   donum quod heri accepi optimum est.
2   videsne pecuniam quae humi iacet?
3   ancilla quam omnes amant pulcherrima est.
4   senex cui epistulam misisti non adest.
5   turba cuius clamores audire possumus irata esse videtur.
6   da mihi equum qui celerior est, imperator!
7   captivi quorum custos eram omnes effugerunt.
8   vulnera quae pro patria passi sumus gravissima erant.
9   hic est liber sine quo nihil facere possum.
10   duces quibus antea credideram fratrem meum non defenderunt.

Less common pronouns

who? what?

		m	*f*	*n*
sg	nom	quis	quis	quid
	acc	quem	quam	quid

(other parts the same as the relative pronoun *qui, quae, quod*: see page 35)

This is used in direct questions (see page 73), where it comes first word in the sentence, and also in indirect questions (see pages 108-9).

Exercise 17   Question pronouns

1   quis pecuniam in silva celavit?
2   quem in foro heri vidisti?
3   cui praemium dedisti, domine?
4   cuius est hic gladius?
5   quid ibi accidit?

a, a certain, *pl* some

		m	*f*	*n*
sg	nom	quidam	quaedam	quoddam
	acc	quendam	quandam	quoddam
	gen	cuiusdam	cuiusdam	cuiusdam
	dat	cuidam	cuidam	cuidam
	abl	quodam	quadam	quodam
pl	nom	quidam	quaedam	quaedam
	acc	quosdam	quasdam	quaedam
	gen	quorundam	quarundam	quorundam
	dat	quibusdam	quibusdam	quibusdam
	abl	quibusdam	quibusdam	quibusdam

This is the relative pronoun *qui, quae, quod* with *-dam* stuck on the end, and minor adjustments. Again note the distinctive genitive and dative singular endings (this time with *-dam* added).

• Compare how *idem* (see page 34) is the pronoun *is, ea, id* with *-dem* stuck on the end. In forming parts of *quidam* too, any part of the original pronoun ending *-m* changes it to *-n* before *-dam* is added, to ease pronunciation (so masculine accusative singular *quendam*, not *quemdam*). Here the neuter ending *-d* is kept, producing *quoddam*.

Any part of *quidam* can be used alone or with a noun (which it usually follows):

> librum quendam quaero.
> I am looking for a certain book.
>
> feminae quaedam in via stabant.
> Some women were standing in the street.

---

		someone, something		
		m	*f*	*n*
sg	*nom*	aliquis	aliqua	aliquid
	acc	aliquem	aliquam	aliquid

(the rest goes like the relative pronoun *qui*, *quae*, *quod*: see page 35)

The nominative and accusative parts of this are like the question pronoun *quis*, *quid* (see page 37) with *ali-* stuck on the front, except that there is a separate feminine form in the nominative. This *ali-* is the adjective/pronoun *alius* used as a prefix.

> aliquem in horto videre possum.
> I can see someone in the garden

An adjective can be added:

> aliquid malum hic accidit.
> Something bad happened here.

Exercise 18   Less common pronouns (i)

1	verba quaedam audire non poteram.
2	aliquis mihi in foro appropinquavit.
3	est femina quaedam quam omnes amamus.
4	aliquos per viam ambulantes vidi.
5	nonne consilium quoddam novum habes?
6	aliqua nobis haec narravit.
7	cenam servi cuiusdam auxilio celeriter parare poteramus.
8	femina cibum alicui dedit.
9	nomina quorundam nemo scit.
10	librum alicuius hic habeo.

one ... the other (*of two*), another, a/the second

		m	f	n
sg	*nom*	alter	altera	alterum
	acc	alterum	alteram	alterum
	gen	<u>alterius</u>	<u>alterius</u>	<u>alterius</u>
	dat	<u>alteri</u>	<u>alteri</u>	<u>alteri</u>
	abl	altero	altera	altero
pl	*nom*	alteri	alterae	altera
	acc	alteros	alteras	altera
		etc	*etc*	*etc*

(regular 2-1-2 plural: see page 16)

Again note the distinctive genitive and dative singular forms. This gives us the English word *alternate*. It is often used in a pair, requiring a different translation each time (*one ... the other*):

> alter liber difficilis est, alter facilis.
> One book is difficult, the other easy.

• Note that *alter* must not be confused with *altus* (= high *or* deep).

The use of *alter ... alter* implies that just two are involved. If there are more than two, *alius ... alius* is used. In the singular this is translated *one ... another*, but it is more often found in the plural as *some ... others*:

> alii servorum laborabant, alii in taberna sedebant.
> Some of the slaves were working, others were sitting in the pub.

• If forms of *alius* different from each other in gender and/or case are paired, a double statement is made (abbreviated in Latin, as it can be in English):

	alii alia de hac re dicunt.
short for	alii alia, alii alia de hac re dicunt.
literally	Some people say some things about this matter, others say other things.
i.e.	Different people say different things about this matter.

the rest, the others (*pl only*)

		m	f	n
pl	*nom*	ceteri	ceterae	cetera
	acc	ceteros	ceteras	cetera
		etc	*etc*	*etc*

(regular 2-1-2 plural: see page 16)

• The English *etc* is an abbreviated form of the neuter plural *et cetera* (= and the other things).

		no-one *m/f*	nothing *n*
sg	*nom*	nemo	nihil (*indeclinable*)
	acc	neminem	
	gen	nullius	
	dat	nemini	
	abl	nullo	

This is formed like a third declension noun (stem *nemin-*), but its genitive and ablative are borrowed from the adjective *nullus* (= no ... , not any).

Note that the distinctive singular endings used by most pronouns (genitive *-ius*, dative *-i* across all three genders) are also used for the following adjectives which are otherwise regular 2-1-2 in declension:

	alius	other, another, else	
	ullus	any	
	nullus	no ... , not any	
	solus	alone, only	
	totus	whole	
also	unus	one	(see page 74)

Exercise 19   Less common pronouns (ii)

1   nemo nomen senis cognovit.
2   ceteris necatis, unus miles domum advenit.
3   neminem in foro conspexi.
4   alii manserunt, alii fugerunt.
5   hic vir rex totius insulae factus est.
6   nonne pecunia in alio loco celata est?
7   pauci militum effugerunt, ceteri capti sunt.
8   alter frater in urbe regit, alter egressus est.
9   libris nostris ablatis, alios emere debemus.
10   tantum praemium nemini dabo.

Prepositions

Prepositions are words such as *in, across, to, from*. As their name (literally *placed in front*) indicates, they come in front of a noun (or pronoun) to express movement or position in relation to it. Prepositions in Latin are followed by either the accusative or the ablative. They serve to focus more closely a meaning the case has already (see pages 3-4 on the accusative, and page 8 on the ablative).

Prepositions with the accusative mostly indicate *motion towards* or *through*, whilst those with the ablative mostly indicate either *a position of rest* in a place or *going away from* it.

(1) Prepositions with the accusative:

ad	to, towards, at
apud	among, with, at the house of
circum	around
in	into
inter	among
per	through, along
post	after
prope	near
sub	under, beneath
trans	across

The additional vocabulary also has:

ante	before, in front of
contra	against
extra	outside
intra	among
praeter	except
propter	on account of, because of

Note that with the name of a town or city (or an island small enough to count as one town) the preposition is omitted, but its name is still accusative if the meaning is motion towards (i.e. it is in the case it would have been in if the preposition *had* been there):

> Romam festinavimus.
> We hurried to Rome.

• The accusative of *domus* (= house, home) is similarly used without a preposition:
> domum ire volo.
> I want to go home.

This must be distinguished from the locative *domi* (= at home): see page 43.

Because a preposition comes just before the noun it refers to, it often displaces an adjective that would otherwise be there, so that the order is *adjective, preposition, noun*:

> multas per vias ambulavimus.
> We walked along many streets.

41

Exercise 20   Prepositions with the accusative

1   omnes cives ad forum festinaverunt.
2   milites circum muros urbis ambulabant.
3   legatus legionis milites in periculum duxit.
4   post cenam dormire volo.
5   Romam mox adveniemus.
6   multas per terras iter feci.
7   pueri prope flumen currebant.
8   frater apud me multos dies manebat.
9   filius regis inter captivos inventus est.
10   hostes trans mare tandem fugerunt.

(2)   Prepositions with the ablative:

a/ab*	from, by
cum	with
de	from, down from; about
e/ex*	from, out of
in	in
pro	in front of, for, in return for
sine	without
sub	under

* The forms *ab* and *ex* are used if the next word starts with a vowel or an *h*. The shorter forms *a* and *e* are used if the next word starts with a consonant.

Note that *a/ab* is also used for the agent with a passive verb: see page 66.

Note that *in* and *sub* are used both with the accusative and with the ablative. In both cases the accusative version implies *motion*, and the ablative implies *position*.

cives in forum ambulabant.
The citizens walked *into* the forum.

cives in foro multas horas stabant.
The citizens were standing *in* the forum for many hours.

We noted that with the name of a town or city (or an island small enough to count as one town) the preposition is omitted (see page 41). The ablative alone here indicates *motion away from*:

Roma discessimus.
We departed from Rome.

The idea of *rest in* such a place is given by a special form of its name called the *locative* (literally *placing*) case, which with a normal singular word is the same as the genitive:

> Romae diu habitabamus.
> We lived in Rome for a long time.

• A few other words also have a locative form:

humi	on the ground	(*from* humus)
domi	at home	(*from* domus; *not like its genitive but formed as if second declension: see pages 10 and 15*)

Exercise 21   Prepositions with the ablative

1	audivistine de morte imperatoris?
2	nihil sine pecunia facere possum.
3	quid sub nave inveniemus?
4	clamores ex omni loco audiebantur.
5	cur in castris manetis?
6	hi pro rege fortiter pugnaverunt.
7	templum multo cum labore tandem confectum est.
8	milites Roma profecti sunt.
9	ille nuntius de monte cucurrit.
10	servus quem sequebamur domi a domino inventus est.

Prefixes and compound verbs

A compound verb has a *prefix* to focus its meaning. Many of the prepositions (pages 41-2) are also used as prefixes to form compound verbs. Note in particular:

a-/ab-	away, from
ad-	to
de-	down, down from
e-/ex-	out of
in-	into, in
re-	back, again
trans-	across

• Attaching the prefix sometimes involves a small modification of spelling, usually to make pronunciation easier:

ab + fero	*becomes*	aufero	I take away, carry off, steal
re + eo		redeo	I go back, come back, return
re + do		reddo	I give back

• The last two are classic examples of *words easily confused* (see pages 115-6): note that *return* works as a translation of *reddo* too in some circumstances (e.g. *I returned his book*).

The prefix and a following preposition often simply reinforce each other, and only one is translated:

> in templum dei ingressi sumus.

literally   We went in into the temple of the god.

i.e.   We went into the temple of the god.

But it is also possible to give two different pieces of information:

> cives in viam exierunt.
>
> The citizens went out (*implying e.g.* from their houses) into the street.

Most compounds are verbs of motion, but note (and distinguish carefully between) the two compounds of *to be*:

> adsum   I am here, I am present
>
> absum   I am away, I am absent   (*perfect* afui)

• Some compounds are more obvious than others. Note the following compounds of *venio* (= I come): *advenio* (= I arrive), *invenio* (= I find, *literally* I come into/upon), and from the additional vocabulary *pervenio* (= I reach, *literally* I come through *implying* obstacles).

• Note that the vowel in the verb stem sometimes changes when a compound is formed: *conficio* (= I finish, *literally* make together) and *interficio* (= I kill, *literally* make among, i.e. put among the dead) are compounds of *facio*; similarly *accipio* (= I receive, literally take to myself) is a compound of *capio*. The compounds of *iacio* (= I throw) shorten the stem to *-icio*: so *deicio* (= I throw down), *eicio* (= I throw out), *inicio* (= I throw in).

• Note that the deponent verb *-gredior* (see page 69) is found *only* in compound forms: so *egredior* (= I go out), *ingredior* (= I enter), *progredior* (= I advance), *regredior* (= I return).

• From the additional vocabulary note (i) *pello* (= I drive) with its compounds *expello* (= I drive out) and *repello* (= I drive back); (ii) *rumpo* (= I burst) with its compounds *irrumpo* (= I burst in, *inr-* changing to *irr-* for ease of pronunciation) and *erumpo* (= I burst out)

Exercise 22   Prefixes and compound verbs

1   pueri libros in flumen iniciebant.
2   omnes senatores nunc adsunt.
3   cives in viam ingressi sunt.
4   puellae prope templum convenerunt.
5   uxor senis diu aberat.
6   servus murum reficere coactus est.
7   quis cibum nostrum abstulit?
8   iuvenis domum redire tandem constituit.
9   multae naves ad portum advenerunt.
10   cur pecuniam meam reddere nolebas?

Conjunctions

A *conjunction* (its name coming from the Latin for *joining together*) connects words or groups of words. Most conjunctions come first word in a sentence or clause. Others, often alternatives with similar meaning, come second word (as if stitching the sentences or clauses together), but are translated first: these are shown with an asterisk.

et	and	et ... et	both ... and
-que	and		
ac *or* atque	and		
sed	but		
tamen*	however	(*similarly* autem* *in the additional vocabulary*)
nam	for	(giving an explanation)
enim*	for		
itaque	and so, therefore		
igitur*	therefore		
priusquam	before	(see pages 75-6 and 105)
postquam	after		

Note that there are three different words for *and*: et can join any words or groups of words. The other two usually join things which are felt to belong together: -que is attached to the end of the second word but translated before it:

> libertus fortis fidelisque erat.
> The freedman was brave and faithful.

If *et* is repeated, it is translated *both* the first time:

> rex et nautas et milites habet.
> The king has both sailors and soldiers.

• Similarly paired are *nec ... nec,* or *neque ... neque* (= neither ... nor): see page 110. Also the pronouns *alter ... alter* and *alii ... alii*: see page 39. For *utrum ... an* (whether ... or) in indirect questions, see page 109. From the additional vocabulary note *aut ... aut* (= either ... or).

Exercise 23   Conjunctions

1   et dominus et servus laetissimi erant.
2   milites nautaeque a rege laudati sunt.
3   cibus atque vinum ibi venduntur.
4   haec insula neque urbes neque flumina habet.
5   uxor militis mortui tristis erat atque tristis manebit.
6   priusquam tu advenisti, ego saepe clamavi sed nemo audivit.
7   mater mea nunc laeta est. domum enim novam habet.
8   nihil accidit. aliam igitur epistulam misi.
9   Romani post bellum gaudebant. mox tamen iterum oppugnati sunt.
10   naves deletae sunt. itaque cives effugere non poterant.

Verbs and conjugations

Endings (see page xii) are particularly important here as they can give several different pieces of information. Take an example:

> festinabamus
> we were hurrying

This word can be broken up into four bits:

(1) festin-	the verb stem meaning *hurry*
(2) -a-	the characteristic vowel for first conjugation (see page 48)
(3) -ba-	the syllable which identifies the imperfect tense (see page 48)
(4) -mus	the basic person ending meaning *we* (see below)

Latin verbs fall into four main patterns called *conjugations* (= joined together, *i.e.* families of verbs). These resemble (and are the origin of) *-er*, *-ir* and *-re* verbs in French. The example verbs used in this book are:

first conjugation	porto	I carry
second	moneo	I warn
third	traho	I drag
fourth	audio	I hear

• Note that some verbs (for example *capio* = I take) are a mixture of third and fourth conjugation. Their present, future and imperfect tenses are the same as fourth conjugation. But because of their infinitive ending *-ere* (see page 50) they count overall as third. The way they form their perfect tense (see pages 54 and 56) is also like third conjugation.

• For further information about conjugations see page 53 on *principal parts*.

Differences in conjugation mainly affect the vowels used within endings. The basic person endings remain the same across all conjugations and across nearly all active tenses (see page 54 for variations in the perfect tense, and page 64 for the conversion from active to passive).

Verbs are usually set out as follows. The numbers 1, 2, 3 refer to persons. First person is *I*, plural *we*. Second person is *you* (both singular and plural: English used to distinguish singular *thou* from plural *ye*). Third person is *he*, *she*, *it*, plural *they*.

BASIC PERSON ENDINGS

sg	*1*	-o *or* -m
	2	-s
	3	-t
pl	*1*	-mus
	2	-tis
	3	-nt

Present tense

conjugation		1st	2nd	3rd	4th
		I carry	I warn	I drag	I hear
sg	1	port-o	mon-eo	trah-o	aud-io
	2	port-as	mon-es	trah-is	aud-is
	3	port-at	mon-et	trah-it	aud-it
pl	1	port-amus	mon-emus	trah-imus	aud-imus
	2	port-atis	mon-etis	trah-itis	aud-itis
	3	port-ant	mon-ent	trah-unt	aud-iunt

The present tense is used to describe an action happening now, though Latin also often uses it to give vividness to a story set in the past, the so-called *historic present* (in English we do this only colloquially, for example in telling a joke).

• The conjunction *dum* (= while) introducing a time clause (see page 76) is always followed by a present tense.

• For the present passive see page 65, and for the present participle see page 80.

Exercise 24   Present tense

1   frater meus Romam ire cupit.
2   puer flumen timet.
3   milites nostri hostes semper vincunt.
4   cur haec arma portatis?
5   omnes custodes nunc dormiunt.
6   tale vinum numquam emo.
7   ille senator civibus persuadet.
8   amici nostri nunc tandem urbi appropinquant.
9   quid consumis, serve?
10   vulnus habeo sed nihil sentio.

Imperfect tense

		I was carrying	I was warning	I was dragging	I was hearing
sg	*1*	port-a-bam	mon-e-bam	trah-e-bam	aud-ie-bam
	2	port-a-bas	mon-e-bas	trah-e-bas	aud-ie-bas
	3	port-a-bat	*etc*	*etc*	*etc*
pl	*1*	port-a-bamus			
	2	port-a-batis			
	3	port-a-bant			

Note the characteristic vowel(s) for each conjugation, immediately after the verb stem:

first	*second*	*third*	*fourth*
a	e	e	ie

These are used in other contexts too: in forming the present participle and gerundive (see pages 80 and 90), and in a slightly different form for the infinitive (see page 50).
The distinctive endings *-bam*, *-bas*, *-bat* make the imperfect tense very easy to recognise.

The word *imperfect* literally means *uncompleted* (not *faulty*, as in modern English). This is because a typical use of the imperfect is to describe an action that was going on when something interrupted it:

> ubi per silvam ambulabamus, corpus mortuum subito invenimus.
> When we were walking through the wood, we suddenly found a dead body.

The imperfect is also used for any action that went on for some time, or was done several times. The translation *was/were* ... is often appropriate, but with some verbs a simple past tense sounds better in English:

> illum equum decem annos habebam.
> I had (*not* was having) that horse for ten years.

• For the imperfect passive see page 65, and for the imperfect subjunctive see page 97.

Exercise 25   Imperfect tense

1   senex nos de periculo viae saepe monebat.
2   multos annos Romae habitabamus.
3   hic servus semper bene laborabat.
4   quid legebas?
5   multis post diebus mari tandem appropinquabamus.
6   milites capti pro vita sua diu orabant.
7   naves Romanorum trans mare lente navigabant.
8   tres dies in castris manebamus; deinde hostes conspeximus.
9   urbem hostium decem annos oppugnabamus.
10 ubi montem ascendebam, flumen subito conspexi.

Future tense

		I shall carry	I shall warn	I shall drag	I shall hear
sg	1	port-a-bo	mon-e-bo	trah-am	aud-i-am
	2	port-a-bis	mon-e-bis	trah-es	aud-i-es
	3	port-a-bit	etc	trah-et	etc
pl	1	port-a-bimus		trah-emus	
	2	port-a-bitis		trah-etis	
	3	port-a-bunt		trah-ent	

Note the two different patterns here. In the imperfect tense all four conjugations use the endings *-bam*, *-bas*, *-bat* etc after their characteristic vowel(s). In the future tense the first and second conjugations do something similar, with the *-bo*, *-bis*, *-bit* endings. You might expect the third and fourth to follow suit, but in fact they use the endings *-am*, *-es*, *-et* etc instead (fourth, and mixed third/fourth, with *i* in front).

The future endings for third conjugation are (except in the first person singular) the same as the present tense endings for second conjugation (*-eo*, *-es*, *-et* etc), so there is a risk of confusion unless you know or look up which conjugation a verb belongs to. Note that in a typical passage (with a story set in the past) the future tense is most likely to be met within direct speech.

• For the future passive see page 65, for the future participle see page 86, and for the future infinitive see page 93.

• For the future perfect see pages 59 and 67.

• For the *hidden future* in time and conditional clauses see pages 76 and 78.

Exercise 26   Future tense

1   omnes liberi regem salutabunt.
2   quid nunc dicam?
3   servi vinum omnibus mox fundent.
4   hostes numquam muros nostros delebunt.
5   multa templa Romae videbimus.
6   quid in nova taberna vendes?
7   urbem nostram semper defendemus.
8   nonne hunc servum fortem liberabis?
9   cenam mox parabo.
10   quam diu dormient hi liberi?

Infinitive

to carry	to warn	to drag	to hear
port-are	mon-ere	trah-ere	aud-ire

The infinitive expresses the basic meaning of the verb: *to do X*. Its name indicates that it is not made *finite* (= restricted) by a person ending. It does however have a tense. This standard infinitive is the *present active* one. There are also perfect and future infinitives, and passive ones: see pages 68 and 93.

Note again (with slight variation from the pattern in the imperfect tense: see page 48) the use of a characteristic vowel for each conjugation, before the *-re*:

first	a
second	e (*long as in* they)
third	e (*short as in* get)
fourth	i

• Note that in the fourth conjugation the characteristic vowel is here *-i-* alone, rather than the combination *-ie-* used for other purposes (see pages 48, 80 and 90).

The infinitive can be sometimes be translated like a noun:

amo currere.
I like running (*literally* I like to run).

Here *running* means *the act of running* (and so is different from the present participle which is an adjective and means *while running*: see page 80).

Exercise 27   Infinitive

1   servum laborare iubebo.
2   num in silva diu manere times?
3   difficile erat nobis verba nuntii audire.
4   pecuniam mihi reddere debes.
5   clamores nostri equos hostium terrere possunt.

The verb *to be*

PRESENT TENSE

I am

sg	*1*	sum
	2	es
	3	est
pl	*1*	sumus
	2	estis
	3	sunt

• Note the similarity to French here (*je suis*, *tu es*, *il est* etc).

IMPERFECT TENSE

I was

sg	*1*	eram
	2	eras
	3	erat
pl	*1*	eramus
	2	eratis
	3	erant

• Note that although this does not use the *-b-* (*-bam* etc) which usually marks the imperfect tense (see page 48), the last part of each ending is still the same.

FUTURE TENSE

I shall be

sg	*1*	ero
	2	eris
	3	erit
pl	*1*	erimus
	2	eritis
	3	erunt

• Note that these tenses of *to be* also have other jobs in Latin. The imperfect and future tenses are used as *sets of endings* to form the pluperfect and (with slight variation) the future perfect of regular verbs: see pages 58-9. The present and imperfect are used as *auxiliary verbs* to form the perfect and pluperfect passive: see page 67.

The verb to be

Note that the verb *to be* takes a *complement* (another noun in the nominative), not an object.

> senex olim miles erat.
> The old man was once a soldier.

Contrast this with:

> senex militem salutavit.
> The old man greeted the soldier.

The verb *to be* can come anywhere in a sentence (it does not have the same preference as other verbs for coming at the end, though it can). If it comes at the beginning of a sentence it is usually translated *there is* etc:

> est taberna in illa via.
> There is a shop in that street.

The infinitive of *sum* is *esse* (= to be).

> volo civis Romanus esse.
> I want to be a Roman citizen.

• Note that the verbs *adsum* (= I am here) and *absum* (= I am away) are *compounds* (see pages 43-4) of *to be* and form their tenses in the same way. The verb *possum* (= I am able) is also a compound of *sum* (see page 60).

• For the perfect tense *fui* (and the pluperfect and future perfect) see pages 56 and 58-9.

Exercise 28   The verb *to be*

1   dux noster severissimus est.
2   illa domus est nostra.
3   num ibi semper tristis eras?
4   est equus in horto.
5   labor difficillimus erat.

Principal parts

This is a system for giving important parts of a verb, from which all other information about it can be worked out. For a regular active verb there are four:

present tense (first person singular)	(see page 47)
infinitive	(see page 50)
perfect tense (first person singular)	(see page 54)
perfect passive participle* (masculine nominative singular)	(see page 82)

* In older and in more advanced books, the fourth principal part is given in a form called the *supine*, which is formed like the *neuter* of the perfect passive participle.

Verbs are commonly quoted with their principal parts in the form:

porto, portare, portavi, portatus   I carry

From this you can tell that the other parts are *to carry, I (have) carried, having been carried*. With regular forms, the principal parts are often abbreviated:

porto, -are, -avi, -atus

As usual with abbreviated Latin words, you remove the last syllable of the first form quoted, then add the alternative endings.

Some verbs do not have the fourth principal part because they cannot be made passive.

• Deponent verbs (see page 69) come into this category (their active perfect participle is used with the auxiliary verb *sum* as the *third* principal part).

Principal parts are a way of plotting information. If just the first person singular of the present tense was quoted, you could not tell a first conjugation verb from a third conjugation one (since both end in *-o*). If just the infinitive was quoted, you could not tell a second conjugation verb from a third conjugation one (since both end in *-ere*, though pronounced differently: see page 50). By seeing all four parts together you can work out all you need to know.

Perfect tense

The word *perfect* in grammar means *completed* (rather than *faultless*: compare *imperfect*, page 48). The perfect tense refers to a completed action in the past. It has its own distinctive endings, but note that all except the first two still fit the basic pattern of person endings (see page 46). Note in particular the distinctive second person forms, both singular and plural: *-isti* and *-istis*.

sg	1	-i
	2	-isti
	3	-it
pl	1	-imus
	2	-istis
	3	-erunt

The endings themselves are the same for all four conjugations. They are added to the *perfect stem*. This is the basic verb stem added to or modified, according to conjugation. First and fourth conjugation verbs normally add a syllable with their characteristic vowel and *-v*:

	present	*perfect stem*
first conjugation	porto	portav-
fourth	audio	audiv-

Many but not all second conjugation verbs add *-u*:

second	moneo	monu-

With the third conjugation it is a bit more complicated. Many verbs add *-s* or a combination of letters involving an *s* sound, but many others are irregular (see the list on page 56). As usual however the common irregular forms quickly become familiar, and looking up or learning the principal parts (see page 53) enables you to work out any perfect tense.

		I (have) carried	I (have) warned	I (have) dragged	I (have) heard
sg	1	port-av-i	mon-u-i	trax-i	aud-iv-i
	2	port-av-isti	mon-u-isti	trax-isti	aud-iv-isti
	3	port-av-it	mon-u-it	trax-it	aud-iv-it
pl	1	port-av-imus	mon-u-imus	trax-imus	aud-iv-imus
	2	port-av-istis	mon-u-istis	trax-istis	aud-iv-istis
	3	port-av-erunt	mon-u-erunt	trax-erunt	aud-iv-erunt

Perfect tense

The perfect tense can be translated *have/has* ... (this is sometimes called a *true* perfect, implying that the effect of the action continues):

> amici nostri advenerunt et in horto sunt.
> Our friends have arrived and are in the garden.

Very often however it is used as what in other languages is called a *simple past* (or *past historic* or *aorist*) for a single action, without *have* ... in English:

> amici nostri advenerunt sed mox discesserunt.
> Our friends arrived but soon left.

Note that the perfect tense of the verb *to be* is *fui*. This is particularly used in the sense *used to be* (implying *but am no longer*):

> servus fui sed nunc libertus sum.
> I was a slave but am now a freedman.

• For *coepi* (= I began) which is a perfect with no equivalent present tense in use, *odi* (= I hate) which is perfect in form but present in meaning, and *inquit* (= he said) which is present in form but usually translated like a perfect tense, see page 63.

• For the perfect passive see page 67.

Exercise 29   Perfect tense (regular forms)

1   omnes cives ad portum festinaverunt.
2   urbem hostium tandem oppugnavimus.
3   puer epistulam in villa celavit.
4   quo heri navigavistis, nautae?
5   nuntius nos de periculo monuit.
6   ancillam novam salutavi.
7   rex advenit et in villa est.
8   quis hos muros aedificavit?
9   custodes qui aderant nihil audiverunt.
10   cur hunc servum liberavisti, domine?

Common irregular perfect tenses

Here are forty of the most important irregular perfect tenses, which should be learned (others can be found in the vocabulary, pages 133-47):

conjugation	verb	perfect tense	meaning
1st	adiuvo	adiuvi	I helped
	do	dedi	I gave
	sto	steti	I stood
2nd	iubeo	iussi	I ordered
	maneo	mansi	I remained, I stayed
	persuadeo	persuasi	I persuaded
	rideo	risi	I laughed
	sedeo	sedi	I sat
	video	vidi	I saw
3rd	ago	egi	I did, I acted
	cogo	coegi	I forced
	curro	cucurri	I ran
	dico	dixi	I said
	discedo	discessi	I departed, I left
	duco	duxi	I led
	frango	fregi	I broke
	intellego	intellexi	I understood
	lego	legi	I read
	mitto	misi	I sent
	pono	posui	I placed, I put
	promitto	promisi	I promised
	quaero	quaesivi	I searched for, I asked for
	relinquo	reliqui	I left
	scribo	scripsi	I wrote
	surgo	surrexi	I got up
	trado	tradidi	I handed over
	traho	traxi	I dragged
	vinco	vici	I conquered, I won
	vivo	vixi	I lived
3rd/4th	accipio	accepi	I received
	capio	cepi	I took, I captured
	conspicio	conspexi	I caught sight of
	facio	feci	I made, I did
	fugio	fugi	I ran away, I fled
	iacio	ieci	I threw
4th	venio	veni	I came
Irregular	eo	i(v)i	I went
	fero	tuli	I carried, I brought
	possum	potui	I was able
	sum	fui	I was

Common irregular perfect tenses

If you note certain patterns in the list of irregular perfect tenses, they are easier to learn.

(1) Change of vowel from present stem, especially *a* to *e*:

ago	egi
frango	fregi
capio	cepi
facio	feci
iacio	ieci

(2) Adding an *s* involves *c* plus *s* being written as *x*, or other similar modification to make the perfect easier to pronounce:

dico	dixi
duco	duxi
intellego	intellexi
mitto	misi
scribo	scripsi

Exercise 30   Irregular perfect tenses (i)

1   omnes cives statim surrexerunt.
2   imperator milites in magnum periculum duxit.
3   quis hanc epistulam scripsit?
4   nuntius regis nihil mihi dixit.
5   multa dona illi seni misimus.
6   quot libros huic puero dedisti?
7   legatus legionis statim discessit.
8   nautae navem in mare traxerunt.
9   quid in bello egisti, pater?
10   pueri per viam celeriter cucurrerunt.

Exercise 31   Irregular perfect tenses (ii)

1   servumne in via conspexisti?
2   hunc senem adiuvimus.
3   puellae omnes riserunt.
4   miles gladios in castra tulit.
5   quis primus in summo monte stetit?
6   femina pecuniam in templo posuit.
7   ille puer nihil dicere potuit.
8   consilium novum quaesivi.
9   dominus servos laborare coegit.
10   puer portam horti fregit.

Pluperfect tense

		I had carried	I had warned	I had dragged	I had heard
sg	*1*	port-av-eram	mon-u-eram	trax-eram	aud-iv-eram
	2	port-av-eras	mon-u-eras	trax-eras	aud-iv-eras
	3	port-av-erat	*etc*	*etc*	*etc*
pl	*1*	port-av-eramus			
	2	port-av-eratis			
	3	port-av-erant			

The perfect stem (see page 54) is used again here. It is followed by the imperfect tense of the verb *to be* (see page 51) used as a set of endings.

Pluperfect literally means *more than perfect*: it refers to something which *had already* happened at a point in the past referred to by a perfect or imperfect tense.

> senex, qui nihil antea audiverat, epistulam brevem accepit.
> The old man, who had heard nothing previously, received a short letter.

The pluperfect refers to something two stages back: if you think of time like a lift in a multi-storey building, the pluperfect is two floors down from the present tense. The translation *had* is always used in English.

Failure to recognise and correctly translate verbs in the pluperfect tense is a very common mistake in GCSE.

• Note that the pluperfect of the verb *to be* is *fueram* (= I had been).

• For the pluperfect passive see page 67, and for the pluperfect subjunctive see page 106.

Exercise 32   Pluperfect tense

1   librum quem olim legeram iterum inveni.
2   militem fortiorem numquam videram.
3   dominus servum qui multos cives servaverat libenter liberavit.
4   senator qui surrexerat iterum sedere constituit.
5   quot hostes necaveras antequam hoc vulnus accepisti?
6   ubi illum cibum comsumpserat, senex mortuus est.
7   Romani antea reges habuerant.
8   ei qui nihil audiverant nihil intellegebant.
9   miles qui montem ascenderat praemium accepit.
10   puer tandem opus fecit quod olim promiserat.

Future perfect tense

		I shall have carried	I shall have advised	I shall have dragged	I shall have heard
sg	*1*	port-av-ero	mon-u-ero	trax-ero	aud-iv-ero
	2	port-av-eris	mon-u-eris	trax-eris	aud-iv-eris
	3	port-av-erit	*etc*	*etc*	*etc*
pl	*1*	port-av-erimus			
	2	port-av-eritis			
	3	port-av-erint			

The perfect stem (page 54) is used again here. It is followed by the future tense of the verb *to be* (see page 51) used as a set of endings, except that the third person plural is *-erint* (because *-erunt* has already been used for the perfect tense).

The future perfect tense refers to a time in the future when something that has not happened yet *will have* happened: it imagines being at a point two stages into the future, and looking back at something one stage into the future. Using again the analogy of the lift in the multi-storey building, this is like going up two floors then looking one floor down.

The future perfect tense is not very common. In time clauses (see page 76) it is a *hidden future*, in Latin expressing very accurately when something will happen but in English better translated as a present or perfect tense:

> ubi frater meus advenerit, salutabo eum.
> *literally* When my brother will have arrived, I shall greet him.
> *i.e.* When my brother arrives (*or* has arrived), I shall greet him.

• Note that the future perfect tense of the verb *to be* is *fuero*.

Exercise 33   Future perfect tense

1   amici nostri qui nunc absunt ante noctem advenerint.
2   ubi cives portas aperuerint, urbem intrabimus.
3   prope mare habitabo ubi villam aedificavero.
4   hic senex mox centum annos vixerit.
5   non dicam priusquam tacueris.

Very irregular verbs

		PRESENT	IMPERFECT	FUTURE	PERFECT
		I am able, I can	I was able, I could	I shall be able	I was/have been able, I could
sg	1	pos-sum	pot-eram	pot-ero	potu-i
	2	pot-es	pot-eras	pot-eris	potu-isti
	3	pot-est	etc	etc	etc
pl	1	pos-sumus			
	2	pot-estis			
	3	pos-sunt			

This is a compound of the verb *to be* (see page 51). It is formed by sticking *pot-* (originally a separate adjective *potis* = able) on the front of the equivalent part of *to be*. Where that starts with *s*, *pot-* changes to *pos-* (producing *ss*) to make it easier to pronounce. In the perfect tense the *f* of *fui* (the perfect of *to be*) disappears for the same reason, so *pot-fui* becomes *potui*. Similarly the pluperfect is *potueram* (= I had been able), and future perfect *potuero* (= I shall have been able).

The verb *possum* is commonly followed by an infinitive:

> hi liberi bene legere possunt.
> These children can read well.

The infinitive of possum is *posse* (= to be able).

• For the imperfect and pluperfect subjunctive of *possum* see pages 97 and 106.

		PRESENT	IMPERFECT	FUTURE	PERFECT
		I go	I was going	I shall go	I went, I have gone
sg	1	eo	ibam	ibo	i(v)i
	2	is	ibas	ibis	i(v)isti
	3	it	ibat	ibit	i(v)it
pl	1	imus	ibamus	ibimus	i(v)imus
	2	itis	ibatis	ibitis	istis *or* ivistis
	3	eunt	ibant	ibunt	i(v)erunt

Note here the similarity to equivalent tenses of regular verbs: four bits of the present tense like the endings for third conjugation (see page 47), imperfect and future endings which are abbreviated versions of regular patterns (see pages 48-9), and regular perfect endings on a perfect stem which can be either *i-* or *iv-* for the perfect tense itself, but is just *i-* in the pluperfect *ieram* (= I had gone) and the future perfect *iero* (= I shall have gone).

The infinitive of *eo* is *ire* (= to go).

Very irregular verbs

The following three verbs should be studied together, noting recurrent features:

		PRESENT	IMPERFECT	FUTURE	PERFECT
		I want	I wanted, I was wanting	I shall want	I (have) wanted
sg	*1*	volo	volebam	volam	volui
	2	vis	volebas	voles	voluisti
	3	vult	*etc*	*etc*	*etc*
pl	*1*	volumus		*pluperfect:*	volueram, volueras *etc*
	2	vultis		*future perfect:*	voluero, volueris *etc*
	3	volunt		*infinitive:*	velle

This is a modified version of third conjugation (in some bits of the present, in the imperfect and in the future: see pages 47-9), though its perfect stem is more like second conjugation (see page 54).

		PRESENT	IMPERFECT	FUTURE	PERFECT
		I do not want	I did not want	I shall not want	I did not want, I have not wanted
sg	*1*	nolo	nolebam	nolam	nolui
	2	non vis	nolebas	noles	noluisti
	3	non vult	*etc*	*etc*	*etc*
pl	*1*	nolumus		*pluperfect:*	nolueram, nolueras *etc*
	2	non vultis		*future perfect:*	noluero, nolueris *etc*
	3	nolunt		*infinitive:*	nolle

This is a compound (see page 43) of *volo*, using the negative *non* (= not) as a prefix. When *non* is stuck on the front of *vol-* it shortens to *nol-*. The same thing does not happen with the irregular bits starting *vu-* or *vi-*, so some bits of the present tense stay as two separate words.

• For the use of the imperative of *nolo* (*noli, nolite*) in a negative direct command see page 71.

		PRESENT	IMPERFECT	FUTURE	PERFECT
		I prefer	I was preferring	I shall prefer	I (have) preferred
sg	*1*	malo	malebam	malam	malui
	2	mavis	malebas	males	maluisti
	3	mavult	*etc*	*etc*	*etc*
pl	*1*	malumus		*pluperfect:*	malueram, malueras *etc*
	2	mavultis		*future perfect:*	maluero, malueris *etc*
	3	malunt		*infinitive:*	malle

This too is a compound of *volo*, using a shortened form of the comparative adverb *magis* (= more) as a prefix: it means *want* something *more* than something else.

Finally note under the heading of irregular verbs *fero*, which is basically third conjugation but loses some vowels from its endings and has unusual principal parts:

PRESENT			ACTIVE	PASSIVE
			I carry	I am carried
sg	*1*		fero	feror
	2		fers	fer(e)ris
	3		fert	fertur
pl	*1*		ferimus	ferimur
	2		fertis	ferimini
	3		ferunt	feruntur

principal parts: fero, ferre, tuli, latus*

imperative:	fer (see page 71), ferte
imperfect:	ferebam, ferebas *etc*
future:	feram, feres *etc*
perfect:	tuli, tulisti *etc*
perfect passive:	latus sum, latus es *etc*

* Note that the following verbs are compounds (see page 43) of *fero*, with similar principal parts:

aufero, auferre, abstuli, ablatus	I take away, I steal	(*au = ab*, away)
offero, offere, obtuli, oblatus	I offer	(*ob* = for)

Note also that the last two parts are found with the prefix *sub-* as the last two principal parts of *tollo*, formed as if it had started *subfero* (which would have the same meaning):

tollo, tollere, sustuli, sublatus   I raise, I lift up

Exercise 34   Very irregular verbs (i)

1   haec verba facile legere possum.
2   quo nunc itis, pueri?
3   frater meus celeriter currere potest.
4   ubi domum ibam clamorem subito audivi.
5   nihil antea intellegere potueram; deinde hunc librum inveni.
6   ubi Romam iero imperatorem salutabo.
7   omnes hi milites fortiter pugnare poterant.
8   in forum mox ibimus.
9   quis in hac insula habitare potest?
10   nemo pecuniam invenire potuit.

Exercise 35   Very irregular verbs (ii)

1   hic senex aliquid dicere vult.
2   mater mea heri exire nolebat.
3   nemo hunc senatorem audire volebat.
4   talem cibum consumere antea nolueram.
5   cur respondere non vis?
6   facilius est velle quam facere.
7   malumus in villa manere quam ad urbem ambulare.
8   quis hunc librum legere volet?
9   quid in villam fertis, servi?
10   cur hic sedere mavis?

Defective and impersonal verbs

(1) A *defective* verb is one of which only a few bits exist.

A very common example is *inquit* (= he says/said). It is normally found only in this third person form (though there is a plural *inquiunt* = they say/said). It is in origin a present tense but is usually translated like a perfect. It is used to quote the actual words of a speaker, which it often interrupts:

> 'ecce' inquit 'amici nostri appropinquant.'
> 'Look!' he said 'our friends are approaching.'

In this example it is effective to keep the same order in English, with *he said* interrupting the quotation. Often however it is better translated first, especially if a subject is given:

> nuntius 'festinate, cives' inquit 'nam hostes urbi appropinquant.'
> The messenger said 'Hurry, citizens, for the enemy are approaching the city.'

• Note carefully that *inquit* means *said* (not *asked*): this is a common mistake in GCSE. The word may coincidentally be used with a question, but it has no connection with the English *inquire*.

Two verbs exist only in perfect tense forms (and the associated pluperfect and future perfect):

	coepi	I have begun, I began	(see page 54)
	coeperam	I had begun	(see page 58)
	coepero	I shall have begun	(see page 59)
infinitive	coepisse	to have begun	(like a perfect infinitive: page 93)

• From the additional vocabulary *incipio* (= I begin) provides a present tense.

The second is similar in form, but the perfect here is *present* in meaning (so the pluperfect is like an imperfect or perfect, and the future perfect like an ordinary future):

	odi	I hate
	oderam	I hated
	odero	I shall hate
infinitive	odisse	to hate

This probably came about because the original idea was *I have come to hate* (a *true perfect*: see page 55), hence *I do hate now*.

(2) An *impersonal* verb is a third person singular, with *it* supplied as the subject:

> placet   it pleases, it suits (+ *dative*)   (2nd conjugation, like *monet*)

> nobis placet haec audire.
> It pleases us to hear these things.

Exercise 36   Defective and impersonal verbs

1. librum longum legere heri coepi.
2. puella 'pueros' inquit 'odi atque semper odero.'
3. prima luce profecti sumus, sed hostes antea fugere coeperant.
4. placetne tibi ad tabernam ire?
5. 'odi' inquit 'et amo.'

Active and passive

With an active verb the grammatical subject is also the person or thing who does the action:

> The boy *kicks* the ball.

With a passive verb the grammatical subject is on the receiving end of the action:

> The ball *is kicked* by the boy.

Passive verbs in Latin are easy to recognise. Most present, imperfect and future active forms can be converted to their passive equivalents by a simple formula. Here are the basic person endings for each:

		active	*passive*
sg	1	-o *or* -m	-r (*added to* -o, *or in place of* -m)
	2	-s	-ris
	3	-t	-tur
pl	1	-mus	-mur
	2	-tis	-mini
	3	-nt	-ntur

The vowel(s) in front of these person endings will usually be the same as in the active. This formula works for the present, imperfect and future tenses. Here are some examples:

present
portas	you (*sg*) carry
portaris	you (*sg*) are being carried

imperfect
monebamus	we were warning
monebamur	we were being warned

future
audient	they will hear
audientur	they will be heard

• The only minor exception to note is that the second person singular of the present tense of third conjugation, and of the future tense of first and second conjugations, is *-eris* in the passive instead of the expected *-iris*:

mittis	you (*sg*) send
mitteris	you (*sg*) are sent

videbis	you (*sg*) will see
videberis	you (*sg*) will be seen

• This formula also works for the passive form of the imperfect subjunctive: see page 97.

• The perfect, pluperfect and future perfect passive are formed in a different way: see page 67.

64

Present, imperfect and future passive

PRESENT PASSIVE

		I am carried	I am warned	I am dragged	I am heard
sg	*1*	portor	moneor	trahor	audior
	2	portaris	moneris	traheris*	audiris
	3	portatur	monetur	trahitur	auditur
pl	*1*	portamur	monemur	trahimur	audimur
	2	portamini	monemini	trahimini	audimini
	3	portantur	monentur	trahuntur	audiuntur

Note that the present passive can be translated *I am being carried* (implying *at this moment*), as well as *I am carried.*

IMPERFECT PASSIVE

		I was being carried	I was being warned	I was being dragged	I was being heard
sg	*1*	portabar	monebar	trahebar	audiebar
	2	portabaris	monebaris	trahebaris	audiebaris
	3	portabatur	*etc*	*etc*	*etc*
pl	*1*	portabamur			
	2	portabamini			
	3	portabantur			

FUTURE PASSIVE

		I shall be carried	I shall be warned	I shall be dragged	I shall be heard
sg	*1*	portabor	monebor	trahar	audiar
	2	portaberis*	moneberis*	traheris	audieris
	3	portabitur	*etc*	trahetur	*etc*
pl	*1*	portabimur		trahemur	
	2	portabimini		trahemini	
	3	portabuntur		trahentur	

As with the future active (page 49), note the distinction between two sets of endings: a passive version of *-bo*, *-bis*, *-bit* for first and second conjugations, and a passive version of *-am*, *-es*, *-et* for third and fourth.

* Note the ending *-eris* instead of the expected *-iris*: see page 64.

Agent and instrument

Consider the following simple sentence (consisting of subject, object and active verb):

> servus dominum necat.
> The slave kills the master.

When this is made passive, the original object becomes the subject, and the original subject becomes the *agent* (the *person by whom* the action is done), expressed by *a* (or *ab* if the next word starts with a vowel or *h-*) and the ablative:

> dominus a servo necatur.
> The master is killed by the slave.

If with a passive verb we are told the *thing with which* the action is done, this is called the *instrument* and is also put in the ablative, but without *a/ab*:

> dominus gladio necatur.
> The master is killed with a sword.

Both agent and instrument can be expressed in the same sentence:

> dominus a servo gladio necatur.
> The master is killed by the slave with a sword.

Exercise 37   Present, imperfect and future passive

1   cibus a pueris consumebatur.
2   hic liber saepe legitur.
3   villa nova mox hic aedificabitur.
4   cur a domino laudabaris?
5   omnes cives clamoribus hostium terrentur.
6   multae epistulae mihi a matre mittebantur.
7   murus ab hostibus nunc deletur.
8   equi in castra a servis ducebantur.
9   vox regis numquam iterum audietur.
10   haec urbs decem annos oppugnabatur.

Perfect, pluperfect and future perfect passive

PERFECT PASSIVE

		I was/have been carried	I was/have been warned	I was/have been dragged	I was/have been heard
sg	1	portatus sum	monitus sum	tractus sum	auditus sum
	2	portatus es	monitus es	tractus es	auditus es
	3	portatus est	*etc*	*etc*	*etc*
pl	1	portati sumus			
	2	portati estis			
	3	portati sunt			

The perfect passive is made up of the *perfect passive participle* (see page 82) with the *present* tense of the verb *to be* (see page 51) used as an auxiliary verb. The present is used because the participle is perfect tense already. The perfect passive literally means *I am in a state of having been carried*, i.e. *I have been carried* or simply *I was carried*. Note that the participle is always nominative, but changes its ending according to the number and gender of the subject.

PLUPERFECT PASSIVE

		I had been carried	I had been warned	I had been dragged	I had been heard
sg	1	portatus eram	monitus eram	tractus eram	auditus eram
	2	portatus eras	monitus eras	tractus eras	auditus eras
	3	portatus erat	*etc*	*etc*	*etc*
pl	1	portati eramus			
	2	portati eratis			
	3	portati erant			

The pluperfect passive is formed in a comparable way. Here the auxiliary verb is the *imperfect* tense of the verb *to be* (see page 51): added to the participle which is perfect tense already, it creates the pluperfect, which is two stages back (see page 58). The pluperfect passive literally means *I was* (already, at some time in the past) *in a state of having been carried*, i.e. *I had been carried*.

FUTURE PERFECT PASSIVE

		I shall have been carried	I shall have been warned	I shall have been dragged	I shall have been heard
sg	1	portatus ero	monitus ero	tractus ero	auditus ero
		etc	*etc*	*etc*	*etc*

The (not very common) future perfect passive is again formed in a comparable way. This time the auxiliary verb is the *future* tense of the verb *to be* (see page 51): literally *I shall be in a state of having been carried*, i.e. *I shall have been carried*. (Often in practice it is translated even more simply like a present tense: see page 59.)

67

Exercise 38   Perfect, pluperfect and future perfect passive

1   servus fortissimus a domino liberatus est.
2   milites qui a rege arcessiti erant omnes postea effugerunt.
3   multa pecunia huic servo data est.
4   dux hostium tandem occisus est.
5   ianua ab ancilla celeriter aperta est.
6   senex a puella adiutus erat, sed postea iterum discessit.
7   pueri domum redire iussi sunt.
8   cena optima nobis a matre parata est.
9   epistula mihi a sorore antea missa erat.
10   verba quae a liberto dicta erant ab omnibus laudata sunt.

Passive infinitive

The forms of the present·*active* infinitive (see page 50) for the four conjugations are:

to carry	to warn	to drag	to hear
port-are	mon-ere	trah-ere	aud-ire

These are made *passive* by changing the final -*e* to -*i*, except that in the third conjugation the -*er*- drops out, so that the passive infinitive ending is just -*i*:

to be carried	to be warned	to be dragged	to be heard
port-ari	mon-eri	<u>trah-i</u>	aud-iri

• Note carefully this unusual formation for the third conjugation, since with some verbs it may look like the first person singular of the perfect tense, or like the dative singular of a related third declension noun. From the additional vocabulary note *rego* (= I rule), with passive infinitive *regi* (= to be ruled), which is the same as the dative of *rex* (= king).

• For further infinitives (perfect active and passive, and future active) see page 93.

• For the use of any type of infinitive in indirect statement see pages 92-6.

Exercise 39   Passive infinitive

1   num hic cibus consumi potest?
2   hic senex a te curari non vult.
3   epistula quam scripsisti statim mitti debet.
4   nonne haec ancilla laudari vult?
5   iubeo omnes servos meos nunc liberari.

Deponent verbs

Deponent verbs are *passive* in form but *active* in meaning: they look as if they are passive, but are actually active (the term *deponent* is not very informative: it literally means *laying aside*, i.e. *not taking up* a passive sense). They are formed like the passive equivalent of each tense, according to their conjugation. Their principal parts (see page 53) therefore look like this:

conor, conari, conatus sum   I try

A deponent verb behaves in a sentence just like an ordinary active one. (Note however that it cannot be *made* passive: it has *only* a passive *form*, but *only* an active *meaning*.)

conjugation	1st	2nd	3rd	4th	
	I try	I seem*	I speak	I rise*	* from the additional vocabulary

only 1st person shown

(like present, future and imperfect passive: see page 65)

present	conor	videor	loquor	orior
imperfect	conabar	videbar	loquebar	oriebar
future	conabor	videbor	loquar	oriar

(like perfect, pluperfect and future perfect passive: see page 67)

perfect	conatus sum	visus sum	locutus sum	ortus sum
pluperfect	conatus eram	visus eram	locutus eram	ortus eram
future perfect	conatus ero	visus ero	locutus ero	ortus ero

(like passive infinitive: see page 68)

infinitive	conari	videri	loqui	oriri

Other deponent verbs:

hortor, hortari, hortatus sum	I encourage, I urge
proficiscor, proficisci, profectus sum	I set out
sequor, sequi, secutus sum	I follow
in/e/re-gredior, -gredi, -gressus sum	I go in/out/back (*also* progredior = I advance)
morior, mori, mortuus sum	I die
patior, pati, passus sum	I suffer, I endure

and from the additional vocabulary:

miror, mirari, miratus sum	I wonder at, I admire
vereor, vereri, veritus sum	I fear, I am afraid (see page 104)
precor, precari, precatus sum	I pray (to)
utor, uti, usus sum	I use (+ *abl*)

• The perfect participle with active meaning (e.g. *locutus* = having spoken) is a useful feature of deponent verbs which does not exist in Latin otherwise. Sometimes it is better translated like a present (e.g. *veritus* = fearing): this must be judged from the context. Deponent verbs also have a present active participle of regular form (e.g. *moriens* = dying): see page 80.

Exercise 40   Deponent verbs

1   haec verba legere diu conabar.
2   imperator milites suos breviter hortatus est.
3   ille senator semper optime loquitur.   (continued ...)

4   frater huius senis mortuus est.
5   prima luce e castris profecti sumus.
6   servus fugit sed custodes celeriter sequebantur.
7   quid tum loquebaris, fili?
8   equus in hortum villae ingressus est.
9   nos omnes vulnera gravissima passi sumus.
10   nuntius mox regredietur.

Semi-deponent verbs

There are only a handful of these. They are active in form in the present, imperfect and future tenses, but become deponent (using the passive forms) in the perfect, pluperfect and future perfect.

		I rejoice *(2nd)*	I become, I am made *(from the additional vocabulary)* *(irregular but similar to 4th conjugation; used as passive of* facio)
PRESENT			
sg	1	gaudeo	fio
	2	gaudes	fis
	3	gaudet	fit
pl	1	gaudemus	-
	2	gaudetis	-
	3	gaudent	fiunt *irregular infinitive* fieri

imperfect	gaudebam	fiebam
future	gaudebo	fiam

(like perfect, pluperfect and future perfect passive: page 67)

perfect	gavisus sum	factus sum
pluperfect	gavisus eram	factus eram
future perfect	gavisus ero	factus ero

• The additional vocabulary also has:

audeo, audere, ausus sum   I dare
soleo, solere, solitus sum   I am accustomed

It is important not to confuse *audeo* with *audio* (= I hear): see page 115.

Exercise 41   Semi-deponent verbs (including words from the additional vocabulary)

1   puella ubi verba nuntii audivit maxime gavisa est.
2   ille puer celeriter currere solebat.
3   post bellum omnes gaudebimus.
4   ego hoc legere numquam ausus sum.
5   quamquam talia facere numquam solitus erat, servus cibum abstulit.

Direct commands

A direct command, telling someone to do something, is expressed by a form of the verb called the *imperative* (from *impero* = I order):

	carry!	warn!	drag!	listen!
sg	port-a	mon-e	trah-e	aud-i
pl	port-ate	mon-ete!	trah-ite!	aud-ite!

Note that the imperative endings for each conjugation use the same vowel as the infinitive (see page 50), except that the third conjugation has *-ite* in the plural.

• Four common third conjugation (or related irregular) verbs drop the *-e* ending in the singular:

dic	say! speak! tell!
duc	lead!
fer	carry!
fac	make! do!

A negative direct command, telling someone *not* to do something, is expressed in a distinctive way. It does not (as you might expect) use a negative with the imperative, but uses the <u>imperative of the irregular verb *nolo*</u> (= I do not want, I am unwilling: see page 61) as a sort of auxiliary verb:

	sg	*pl*
imperatives of nolo:	noli	nolite

This is followed by the *infinitive* of the verb expressing what is not to be done:

negative command:	noli festinare nolite festinare
literally	Be unwilling to hurry!
i.e.	Do not hurry!

• An imperative is often found with a vocative: see page 3.

• For indirect or reported commands (e.g. *I told him to go away*) see page 100.

Exercise 42   Direct commands

1	da mihi illam pecuniam, serve!
2	tacete omnes!
3	urbem fortiter defendite, milites!
4	eicite hos pueros!
5	noli auxilium talibus hominibus dare!
6	vende hunc equum, domine!
7	duc me ad ducem tuum!
8	in forum festinate, cives!
9	nolite domi narrare quod hic audivistis!
10	cibum fer! cenam fac!

Direct questions

A direct question, like a direct command, quotes the actual words of a speaker and ends with a question mark. It is important to distinguish two basic types:

(1) Questions asking if something is the case, to which the answer will be *Yes* or *No*. Any sentence can be made into a question by adding a question mark:

> equum habes?
> Do you have a horse?

More commonly the question is signalled by adding *-ne* to the end of the first word:

> equumne habes?

• Compare how *-que* (= and) is similarly added to the end of another word (see page 45). Adding *-ne* may make a familiar word look strange:

> tene ibi vidi?
> Did I see you there?

• This *-ne* must be carefully distinguished from the negative *ne* (= not, so as not to): see page 110.

A question can be slanted to suggest that the speaker expects a particular answer by using *nonne* (*non* plus *ne*: *literally* is it not the case that? *i.e.* surely?) or *num* (surely ... not?):

> nonne equum habes?
> Surely you have a horse?
> *or*   Don't you have a horse?   (*expecting* Yes)
>
> num equum habes?
> Surely you don't have a horse?   (*expecting* No)

• This use of *num* must be carefully distinguished from its use to mean *whether* in an indirect question (see pages 108-9 and 113).

Exercise 43   Direct questions (with *ne, nonne, num*)

1   regemne vidisti?
2   nonne hoc iter difficile erit?
3   num totum diem dormiebas?
4   gladium habes?
5   gravissimumne est vulnus imperatoris?
6   nonne hunc librum legistis, pueri?
7   tune clamorem audivisti?
8   num talem cibum amas?
9   servine estis?
10   nonne navem conspexistis, cives?

(2) A question asking for specific information is introduced by one of the following question words:

cur	why?
quam	how?
quo modo	how? in what way?
ubi	where?
quo	where to?
unde	where from?
quis, quid	who? which? what?
quantus -a -um	how big?
quot	how many?
qualis -e	what sort of?

Note how most of these begin *qu-* (and an older spelling of *cur* was *quor*): this corresponds to the *wh-* of many equivalent words in English.

Most of these words are adverbs (*quo modo* is an ablative phrase used as an adverb). See page 37 for declension of the pronoun *quis, quid*. The last three are adjectives: *quantus* is regular 2-1-2 in declension (see page 16), *quot* is indeclinable, and *qualis* is third declension like *fortis* (see page 17).

• Note carefully the distinction between the plural of *quantus*, and *quot*:

> quantas naves habetis?
> What size of ships do you have?

> quot naves habetis?
> How many ships do you have?

• Note that *quam* can also introduce an *exclamation*:

> quam fortis es.
> How brave you are!

Exercise 44   Direct questions (asking for specific information)

1   cur tam diu aberatis, amici?
2   quem in horto heri vidisti, senex?
3   quo festinatis, cives?
4   ubi sunt feminae quas custodiebas?
5   unde venit hic servus?
6   quid in illa urbe post bellum accidit?
7   quot servos habes, et quantam villam?
8   qualem cibum mavis?
9   quis necavit militem qui nos servaverat?
10   quo modo hoc facere poterimus?

Numerals

unus, una, unum	one
duo, duae, duo	two
tres, tria	three
quattuor	four
quinque	five
sex	six
septem	seven
octo	eight
novem	nine
decem	ten
centum	100
mille, *pl* milia	1000

• Note also the following adjective (regular 2-1-2 in declension: see page 16):

primus -a -um   first

Numbers above three are indeclinable, except that *mille* has a plural. Declensions of the small numbers are:

	one			
	m	*f*	*n*	
nom	unus	una	unum	(note that *unus* is modifed 2-1-2,
acc	unum	unam	unum	with genitive and dative like a
gen	unius	unius	unius	pronoun: see pages 16 and 28)
dat	uni	uni	uni	
abl	uno	una	uno	

	two			three	
	m	*f*	*n*	*m/f*	*n*
nom	duo	duae	duo	tres	tria
acc	duos	duas	duo	tres	tria
gen	duorum	duarum	duorum	trium	trium
dat	duobus	duabus	duobus	tribus	tribus
abl	duobus	duabus	duobus	tribus	tribus

Exercise 45   Numerals

1   mille milites decem annos fortiter pugnabant.
2   dominus cum tribus ancillis Romam iter fecit.
3   duas sorores habeo.
4   senex quattuor filiorum pater est.
5   pedes unius equi vulnerati erant.

Time expressions

Time *how long* is expressed by the *accusative*:

> multas horas manebamus.
> We stayed for many hours.

> totam noctem dormire volo.
> I want to sleep for the whole night (*or* all night)

Time *when* or *within which* is expressed by the *ablative*:

> Romam illo die tandem vidimus.
> On that day we finally saw Rome.

> milites prima luce profecti sunt.
> The soldiers set out at first light (*or* at dawn).

> amicus meus tribus diebus adveniet.
> My friend will arrive within three days.

• Some prepositions (see page 41) are used in expressions of time:

> per decem annos ibi pugnabamus.
> *literally* We were fighting there through ten years (i.e. for ten whole years)

Here the use of *per* is a bit more emphatic than the accusative alone.

> post cenam librum legi.
> After dinner I read a book.

Here *post* as usual takes the accusative. Note however:

> multis post annis vicimus.
> After many years we were victorious.

Here instead of *post* being a preposition with the accusative, it is used as an adverb (*literally* afterwards by many years). Except in phrases like this, the adverb is usually *postea* (see below).

Note the important distinction between:

post cenam	after dinner	*preposition*	(see page 41)
postea	afterwards	*adverb*	(see page 23)
postquam	after X happened, ...	*conjunction*	(see page 45)

• The adverb *postea* is in origin *post* (the preposition) plus *ea* = these things (neuter accusative plural of *is, ea, id*: see page 28). The conjunction *postquam* means literally *after than*, and introduces a subordinate time clause (see page 76): at a later time *than* one thing happened, a second thing happened.

Exercise 46   Time expressions

1   feminae murum tres dies fortissime custodiebant.
2   templum novum illo anno aedificatum est.
3   fratres mei paucis diebus advenient.
4   Romani hostibus multos annos resistebant.
5   per totam noctem ibi manebamus; prima luce flumen transire conati sumus.
6   post mortem uxoris, senex tristis erat.
7   haec pecunia quinque annos in terra celata erat.
8   decem post annis urbem hostium tandem cepimus.
9   tribus diebus auxilium accipere spero.
10   duae legiones eodem die advenerunt.

Time clauses

Clauses expressing *when* something happens are normally straightforward to translate and have an ordinary indicative verb. They are introduced by words such as:

dum	while
ubi	when
ubi primum	as soon as (*literally* when first)
simulac (*or* simulatque)	as soon as (*literally* at the same time as)
postquam	after
priusquam	before

• Note that *ubi* can also mean *where*, either in a question (see page 73) or introducing a clause stating where something happens (see also page 113).

To give a vivid sense of two things happening simultaneously, *dum* meaning *while* is always followed by a present tense, translated as an imperfect if the action took place in the past:

dum per silvam ambulo, pecuniam inveni.
literally   While I am walking through the wood, I found some money.
i.e.   While I was walking through the wood, I found some money.

• This is a sort of automatic historic present (see page 47), or it could be compared to the way a present participle is used, its tense being in relation to that of the main verb (see page 81).

A time clause referring to the future usually has a *hidden* future verb (a future or future perfect tense expressing accurately when the action happens, but translated as a present):

ubi Roman advenero, apud te manebo.
literally   When I shall have arrived in Rome, I shall stay with you.
i.e.   When I arrive in Rome I shall stay with you.

• For the use of *cum* with a subjunctive verb expressing *when* with a suggestion also of *because*, see page 107. For *dum* with a subjunctive verb meaning *until*, and for *antequam* with a subjunctive verb expressing *before something could* happen, see page 105.

Exercise 47   Time clauses

1   cives, simulac clamores audiverunt, in forum cucurrerunt.
2   postquam epistulam tuam accepi miserrimus eram.
3   dum per terram hostium iter facimus saevissime oppugnati sumus.
4   priusquam a te doctus sum nihil intellegebam.
5   ubi Romam advenio semper laetus sum.

Because and *although* clauses

Like time clauses, these are generally straightforward to translate and have ordinary indicative verbs. They are introduced by:

quod   because
quamquam   although

Both describe circumstances and reasons: *because* gives a reason why something happens, *although* gives a reason why it might have been expected not to.

quod severus est, dominus a servis timetur.
Because he is strict, the master is feared by his slaves.

quamquam severus est, dominus a servis amatur.
Although he is strict, the master is loved by his slaves.

• For the various meanings of *quod* see page 113. For the use of *cum* with a subjunctive verb to mean *since* (strictly for a *suggested* reason, but often not much different from the use of *quod* here) see page 107.

Exercise 48   *Because* and *although* clauses

1   duci nostro credimus quod fortissimus est.
2   quamquam bene laboravi, nullum praemium accepi.
3   puer timebat quod librum incenderat.
4   quod pecuniam non habeo, cibum emere non possum.
5   quamquam fortis es, hostes timere cogeris.

If clauses (conditionals)

A clause containing *si* (= if) is known as a *conditional*, because it sets a condition: if one thing is true, something else follows. Simple conditionals translate naturally into English:

> si tu laetus es, ego quoque gaudeo.
> If you are happy, I too am pleased.

A future conditional has a *hidden* future verb (a future or future perfect translated as a present tense), as in a time clause (see page 76):

> si hunc librum legeris, omnia intelleges.
> *literally*   If you will have read this book, you will understand everything.
> *i.e.*   If you read this book, you will understand everything.

The *if* clause can come anywhere in the sentence:

> servus stultus erat si hoc fecit.
> The slave was stupid if he did this.

The other part of the sentence is typically a stement, but can be for example a command (see page 71):

> si librum meum habes, statim redde.
> If you have my book, give it back at once!

A negative conditional uses *nisi*, which can be translated either *if not* or *unless*:

> nisi ianuam aperies, domum incendam.
> If you do not open the door, I will set the house on fire.
> *or*   Unless you open the door, I will set the house on fire.

Exercise 49   *If* clauses

1   si haec dicis, stultus es.
2   si ad urbem veneris, te libenter salutabo.
3   si captivos necavistis, scelesti estis.
4   si me Romam ire vis, pecuniam mitte!
5   si bene laboratis, nos omnes gaudemus.
6   tristis ero nisi te videbo.
7   si puer hoc fecit, fortissimus erat.
8   si pecuniam meam habes, statim mihi redde!
9   laetus sum si cibum vinumque habeo.
10   nisi viam mox inveniam, domum redire numquam potero.

Connecting relative

A connecting relative is the relative pronoun (see page 35) used to start a new sentence (or a new clause after a semi-colon, which is virtually a new sentence). The appropriate translation here is not the usual *who/which* but (according to number, gender and context) for example *he, she, it, they, these things*: the trick is to identify the part of the relative pronoun that is being used, then think of and translate the equivalent bit of *is, ea, id* (see page 28) or *hic, haec, hoc* (see page 31).

> ancilla tandem advenit. quam ubi vidi, laetissimus eram.
literally The slave-girl finally arrived. Whom when I saw, I was very happy
i.e. The slave-girl finally arrived. When I saw <u>her</u>, I was very happy.

> rex nuntios misit; qui cum advenissent totam rem nobis narraverunt.
literally The king sent messengers. Who when had arrived, they told us the whole story.
i.e. The king sent messengers. When <u>they</u> had arrived, they told us the whole story.

The connecting relative is very common and it is important to be able to recognise it. It is often found as part an ablative absolute (see pages 87-9) or a *cum* clause (see page 107) beginning the new sentence. Because the relative pronoun needs to come first word in the new sentence, some adjustment of word order may be needed in English.

Particular care is needed with *quam* and *quod* because they have several different meanings (see page 113). Only context and sense enable you to tell whether *quod* starting a sentence is a connecting relative or *because* (see page 77).

Note also that *quod* as a connecting relative can be used without a particular neuter word as antecedent, instead referring more loosely to the whole of the previous sentence:

> milites nostri omnes effugerunt. quod ubi vidimus, laetissimi eramus.
literally Our soldiers all escaped. Which (thing) when we saw, we were very happy.
i.e. Our soldiers all escaped. When we saw <u>this</u>, we were very happy.

Exercise 50   Connecting relative (numbers 6-10 include ablative absolute or *cum* clause)

1   hanc puellam olim cognoveram. quam heri iterum conspectam libenter salutavi.
2   nullum cibum habet hic senex; cui volo te cenam optimam parare.
3   a servo fideli servatus sum; quem postea laudatum laete liberavi.
4   imperator noster novum consilium habet. quod ubi audiveritis, omnes gaudebitis.
5   milites fortiter pugnantes vidi. qui, postquam hostes vicerunt, ad regem misi sunt.
6   puer a te missus tandem advenit. cuius verbis auditis viam invenire poteramus.
7   nuntius verba imperatoris nuntiavit. quae cum audivissent, cives gavisi sunt.
8   princeps fratrem diu oderat. quo postea necato multo crudelior erat.
9   rex militem quendam dona ferentem Romam misit. qui cum advenisset, senatoribus totam rem narravit.
10   novus imperator promisit se multa pro civibus facturum esse. quibus confectis etiam carior eis erat.

Present active participle

A *participle* is an adjective formed from a verb. It has characteristics of both: it has endings showing number, gender and case like an adjective, and has a tense (and may have an object) like a verb.

Most Latin verbs have three participles:

present active	*e.g.*	portans	carrying	
perfect passive		portatus	(having been) carried	
future active		portaturus	about to carry	

		carrying		
		m/f		*n*
sg	*nom*	portans		portans
	acc	portant-em		portans
	gen	portant-is		
	dat	portant-i		
	abl	portant-e*		
pl	*nom*	portant-es		portant-ia
	acc	portant-es		portant-ia
	gen	portant-ium		
	dat	portant-ibus		
	abl	portant-ibus		

* The ablative singular is *-e* in ablative absolute (see pages 87-9), but *-i* if used purely as an adjective.

The model for this is a third declension adjective like *ingens* (see page 17), using in the first part of the ending the characteristic vowel(s) for the conjugation (see page 48). Because that vowel is *e* for second and third conjugation, their present participles decline just like *ingens* (except for the variant ablative singular noted above). First conjugation has *-a-* in the first part of the ending as shown above, and fourth has *-ie-*. Thus:

		2nd	3rd	4th
		warning	dragging	hearing
		m/f	*m/f*	*m/f*
sg	*nom*	monens	trahens	audiens
	acc	monentem	trahentem	audientem
		etc	*etc*	*etc*

• Deponent verbs (see page 69) have a present active participle of normal form, e.g. *conans* (= trying).

Present active participle

• Note carefully the unusual present participle of the irregular verb *eo* = I go (see page 60): nominative *iens* (as you might expect), but then stem *eunt-*, so accusative singular *euntem*.

The literal translation of the present active participle is *(while) X-ing*. The tense of any participle tells us when the action happens *in relation to the main verb of the sentence*. Thus a present participle with a past main verb describes two things happening simultaneously in the past:

> exiit ridens.
> He went out laughing.

> pueros cibum consumentes vidimus.
> We saw the boys eating the food.

In these examples the translation *-ing* sounds fine in English, but often the participle is better expanded into a clause introduced by *when* or *while*. If the main verb is past (as it usually is in a passage) the present participle comes out like an imperfect tense (whose person also comes from the main verb):

> per viam ambulantes, clamorem audivimus.
> While we were walking along the road, we heard a shout.

Any participle, like any adjective, can be used as a noun (supplying from the context a word such as *people*). The present participle is often used like this in the genitive plural, and can be difficult to recognise:

> turba salutantium adest.
> *literally* A crowd of greeting ones is here.
> *i.e.* A crowd of people offering greetings is here.

Exercise 51   Present active participle

1   amicos ridentes audivimus.
2   puella fugiens non visa est.
3   puerum cenam consumentem conspexi.
4   filia senis morientis miserrima est.
5   senator ad forum ambulans nihil in via vidit.
6   nautas proficiscentes hortatus sum.
7   videsne illos senes in horto sedentes?
8   strepitus puerorum clamantium saepe ibi auditur.
9   cibum militi laboranti dedi.
10   verba imperatoris turbam audientium terruerunt.

Perfect passive participle

This is the most common participle, and one of the most important building-blocks in Latin grammar.

		m	*f*	*n*
		(having been) carried		
sg	*nom*	portat-us	portat-a	portat-um
	acc	portat-um	portat-am	portat-um
		etc	*etc*	*etc*

(regular 2-1-2: see page 16)

The perfect passive participle is the fourth of the principal parts (see page 53). It may be regular or irregular in formation, according to conjugation:

first	-atus
second	often -itus *(like fourth), but some irregular*
third	*mostly irregular, and need to be learned*
fourth	-itus

2nd	*3rd*	*4th*
(having been) warned	(having been) dragged	(having been) heard
monitus -a -um	tractus -a -um	auditus -a -um

A list of important irregular perfect passive participles is given on page 84.

• The perfect passive participle is used to form several other important pieces of grammar (see pages 67 and 93):

perfect passive	portatus sum	I was carried
pluperfect passive	portatus eram	I had been carried
perfect passive infinitive	portatum esse	to have been carried

Again the tense of the participle is in relation to the main verb. The literal sense *having been X-ed* usually sounds awkward in English and is better avoided. Just *X-ed* is often fine:

> hostes victi lente discesserunt.
> The defeated enemy slowly left.

This use of *defeated* must of course be distinguished in English from its use as a simple past tense (e.g. *we defeated them*).

Because this participle is passive, it can have an agent and/or instrument like any passive verb (see page 66):

> epistulam a senatore missam numquam accepi.
> I never received the letter sent by the senator.

The perfect passive participle is often better replaced by a clause beginning *when*, *after* or *who/which*. Because it refers to something that has already been done when the action described by the main verb happens, it will come out as a *pluperfect* if the main verb is in a past tense. (Compare how a present participle comes out as an imperfect: see page 81).

> milites urbem ab hostibus oppugnatam intraverunt.
> The soldiers entered the city which had been attacked by the enemy.

Exercise 52   Perfect passive participle

1   puer de pecunia celata nihil dixit.
2   muri a deis aedificati numquam delebuntur.
3   cives clamoribus territi dormire non poterant.
4   feminam conspectam salutavi.
5   nonne epistulas ab amico tuo missas iam habes?
6   senex servo vocato librum dedit.
7   nautam e nave eiectum tandem servavi.
8   domum ab hostibus incensam vidimus.
9   per ianuam apertam intravit regina ipsa.
10   verba scripta manent.

Common irregular perfect passive participles

Here are thirty of the most important irregular perfect passive participles, which should be learned (others can be found in the vocabulary, pages 133-47):

participle		meaning	present tense
actus -a -um*	(having been)	done	ago
captus	etc	taken, captured	capio
cognitus		found out	cognosco
coactus		forced	cogo
conspectus		noticed, caught sight of	conspicio
deletus		destroyed	deleo
datus		given	do
ductus		led	duco
factus		made, done	facio
latus		carried	fero
fractus		broken	frango
fusus		poured	fundo
iactus		thrown	iacio
interfectus		killed	interficio
inventus		found	invenio
iussus		ordered	iubeo
lectus		read	lego
missus		sent	mitto
motus		moved	moveo
occisus		killed	occido
oblatus		offered	offero
positus		placed, put	pono
promissus		promised	promitto
quaesitus		looked for	quaero
raptus		seized	rapio
relictus		left	relinquo
scriptus		written	scribo
versus		turned	verto
visus		seen	video
victus		conquered	vinco

* all are regular 2-1-2 in declension (see page 16)

Perfect active participle (from deponent verbs)

Deponent and semi-deponent verbs (see pages 69-70) have a perfect active participle. Examples:

deponent

conatus -a -um	having tried	conor
hortatus	having encouraged	hortor
in/e/re-gressus	having gone in/out/back	in/e/re-gredior
progressus	having advanced	progredior
locutus	having spoken	loquor
mortuus	having died	morior
passus	having suffered	patior
profectus	having set out	proficiscor
secutus	having followed	sequor

semi-deponent

gavisus	having rejoiced	gaudeo

Because a perfect active participle is not otherwise available in Latin, this is a useful feature of deponent verbs (see pages 87-9 on ablative absolute).

Again the literal translation *having X-ed* often sounds artificial, and a translation such as *after doing X* or *when they had done X* is often appropriate. (For the way in which a perfect participle comes out like a pluperfect tense when translated as a clause, see page 83.)

• The perfect tense of a deponent verb is like the perfect passive of an ordinary verb (see pages 67 and 69), consisting of the perfect participle with the auxiliary verb *to be*:

> rex mortuus est.
> The king died (*or* has died).

But it is also possible to read this as simply an adjective with a present tense verb:

> The king is dead.

Exercise 53   Perfect active participle (from deponent verbs)

1   hostes regressi castra sua intraverunt.
2   multas horas locutus senator tandem tacuit.
3   nautae prima hora profecti mox ad portum advenerunt.
4   multa vulnera passus miles mortuus est.
5   milites portas urbis intrare frustra conati abierunt.

Future active participle

		about to carry		
		m	*f*	*n*
sg	*nom*	portat-ur-us	portat-ur-a	portat-ur-um
	acc	portat-ur-um	portat-ur-am	portat-ur-um
		etc	*etc*	*etc*

(regular 2-1-2: see page 16)

This is *formed from* the perfect passive participle, inserting *-ur-* between the stem and the ending, but is *active* in meaning. Similarly for the other conjugations:

2nd	*3rd*	*4th*
about to warn	about to drag	about to hear
moniturus -a -um	tracturus -a -um	auditurus -a -um

There is a whole range of possible translations for the future active participle: *about to ... , going to ... , intending to*. There is often a suggestion of purpose. Like other participles, the future active one is often better translated as a clause (for example *when ...). Like other participles too, its tense is in relation to that of the main verb, so with a passage set in the past a future participle may come out as (for example) <u>*when they were*</u> *about to do X.*

The future active participle is similarly used with the imperfect tense of the auxiliary verb *to be* (see page 51) to form a 'made up' finite tense expressing *future in the past* (contrast future perfect, which is past in the future: page 59). Using again the analogy of the lift in the multi-storey building, this is going two floors down then looking one up: at some point in the past, something *was going to* happen.

> senex pecuniam celaturus erat.
> The old man was going to hide the money.

• The future participle is used with the infinitive of the verb *to be* to form the future infinitive (see page 93).

• Deponent verbs have a future active participle of normal form, e.g. *conaturus* = about to try.

Exercise 54   Future active participle

1   morituri te salutamus.
2   nuntius verba imperatoris narraturus omnes tacere iussit.
3   talem cibum numquam dormiturus consumo.
4   milites urbem oppugnaturi signum exspectabant.
5   epistulam difficilem scripturus diu cogitabam.

Disentangling participles

Any kind of participle within a sentence is often better taken out and translated as a subordinate clause, or even made into a separate main clause joined by *and*:

>pater filiae ex urbe discessurae pecuniam dedit.
>The father gave money to his daughter who was about to leave the city.

>servus vinum fusum mihi dedit.

literally The slave gave the poured wine to me.

but in better English

>The slave gave me the wine which he had poured.

or The slave poured the wine and gave it to me.

In the second example it is assumed from the context that the wine has been poured by the slave rather than someone else, so the passive participle can be translated by an active verb (see page 88 for this point in relation to ablative absolute).

Exercise 55   Disentangling participles

1   milites urbem tandem captam incenderunt.
2   dominus servum in urbem ductum vendidit.
3   hominem gladio tam graviter vulneratum nemo adiuvare potest.
4   senex uxori cibum offerenti nihil dixit.
5   servus omnia audita senatori nuntiavit.

Ablative absolute

This is a phrase consisting of a noun (or pronoun) and participle in the ablative, not linked grammatically with the rest of the sentence. Its name comes from the old sense of *absolute* as *separated* (rather than its modern meaning of *complete*). It is found most commonly with the perfect passive participle, but it can be used with any participle. It describes circumstances which apply when the main action of the sentence happens.

The literal translation *with* ... is sometimes acceptable:

>naves omnibus civibus spectantibus profectae sunt.
>The ships set out with all the citizens watching.

Sometimes words such as *with* and *having been* can be left out, but the phrase still translated literally:

>his rebus factis, senatores discesserunt.
>These things done, the senators left.

More often it is better (as with other participle phrases) to translate an ablative absolute with a clause. The usual point applies about the tense of the participle being in relation to the tense of the main verb.

> rege locuturo omnes tacuerunt.
> When (*or* Because) the king was about to speak, everyone was silent.

When the ablative absolute contains a perfect passive participle, you need to think carefully about whether to make it into an active verb in English, or leave it passive. Consider two examples:

> his verbis auditis, puellae laetissimae erant.
> *literally* With these words having been heard the girls were very happy.

Because it is natural to assume from the context that the girls (rather than someone else) had heard the words, it is appropriate to translate:

> When they had heard these words, the girls were very happy.

Contrast this sentence:

> urbe capta cives miserrimi erant.
> *literally* With the city having been captured the citizens were very miserable.

Here the citizens have obviously not done the capturing (their enemy has), so the translation of the ablative absolute needs to leave it passive:

> Because (*or* When) the city had been captured, the citizens were very miserable.

An ablative absolute commonly comes at the beginning of a sentence. It may be separated off by a comma. It often incorporates a connecting relative (see page 79).

> quo audito, omnes senatorem laudaverunt.
> *literally* With which (thing) having been heard, they all praised the senator.
> *i.e.* When they had heard this, they all praised the senator.

The verb *to be* does not have a present participle, so ablative absolute phrases are sometimes found in which *being* needs to be supplied as the literal translation (and no actual participle is in the sentence):

> Caesare duce hostes vicimus.
> *literally* With Caesar being leader we conquered the enemy.
> *or in better English*
> With Caesar as leader ... *or* Under Caesar's leadership ...

• If a noun referring to a person is in the ablative without a preposition, it is very likely to be an ablative absolute.

• A participle phrase is only put in the ablative absolute if it cannot go into any other case which would relate it to the rest of the sentence. Sometimes a phrase which looks like an ablative absolute is actually dative:

> puellis auxilium petentibus cibum dedi.
> I gave food to the girls who were seeking help.

• Conversely, a participle phrase may be ablative (for example because it follows a preposition), but not ablative absolute:

> nihil scio de femina lacrimanti.
> I know nothing about the woman who is weeping.

Note here that the participle has the ablative singular ending *-i* rather than *-e* because it is being used purely as an adjective (see pages 17 and 80), whereas in an ablative absolute the participle is doing a job like that of a verb in a clause, and has the ablative ending *-e*.

• The fact that ablative absolutes are commonly translated by clauses beginning *who* ... , *when* ... , *because* ... etc illustrates how Latin can express the same meaning in different ways. So for example *his verbis dictis* followed by a third person singular verb means the same as *cum haec dixisset* (= when he had said this): see page 107.

Exercise 56   Ablative absolute

1   his verbis dictis, nuntius discessit.
2   regina horto deleto tristissima erat.
3   militibus paratis imperator proficisci constituit.
4   servis venditis cenam ipse paro.
5   senatore locuto, cives gaudebant.
6   puella laetior erat epistula lecta.
7   hostibus visis omnes timebamus.
8   cives clamoribus auditis auxilium statim miserunt.
9   imperatore mortuo novum ducem invenire debemus.
10   pueris tacere iussis senex villam intravit.

Gerundives

A *gerundive* is an adjective made from a verb. It is not counted as a participle but has similar characteristics. Its literal meaning is *needing to be X-ed* (though this usually needs to be adapted in translation): it is *passive* and has the idea of *necessity*. It does not have a tense, but refers to a sort of possible or hypothetical future (just as an imperative does: see page 71) - something that has not happened yet, but should. It is formed from the verb stem, the characteristic vowel(s) for the conjugation (see page 48) and *-ndus* (with normal 2-1-2 endings: see page 16). Thus:

portandus -a -um	needing to be carried
monendus -a -um	needing to be warned
trahendus -a -um	needing to be dragged
audiendus -a -um	needing to be heard

It is easy to recognise because few other Latin words have the combination of letters *-nd-* with vowels either side.

• The word *gerundive* itself comes from the gerundive of *gero* (a few verbs have the older spelling *-undus* instead of *-endus*), meaning *needing to be performed*. The English word *agenda* is the neuter plural gerundive of *ago*, meaning *things to be done*: the business of a meeting.

The gerundive has three main jobs:

(1) As an adjective, usually with the verb *to be*. Like any adjective it agrees with its noun in number, gender and case.

> urbs delenda est.
> *literally* The city is needing to be destroyed.
> *i.e.* The city must be destroyed.

• Note that *to be destroyed* would work here to represent the gerundive in English, but this must be distinguished from the use of the same phrase to translate a passive infinitive (see page 68).

If a person is put in as the agent, it goes in the *dative* (not *ab* with the ablative, as with ordinary passive verbs: see page 66).

> urbs nobis delenda est.
> *literally* The city is for us (*or* as far as we are concerned) needing to be destroyed.
> *i.e.* The city must be destroyed by us.
> *or (converting to active)*
> We must destroy the city.

Note that the conversion into an active verb in English is only possible if an agent is expressed.

The verb *to be* can be in any tense:

> ille liber mihi legendus erat.
> I had to read that book.

(2) With *ad* to express purpose. This use of *ad* for an aim is an extension of its normal idea of *motion towards*.

> misit nuntios ad regem necandum.
>
> *literally*   He sent messengers (with a view) to the king needing to be killed.
> *i.e.*   He sent messengers to kill the king.

With this use of the gerundive the English translation should get away both from the passive and from the idea of necessity. This may seem a complex change, but if you think of the basic sense of each word (*ad* = to, *necare* = kill, *rex* = king), taking the noun as the object of the verb expressed by the gerundive, the meaning should be obvious.

> domum festinavi ad pecuniam quaerendam.
> I hurried home to look for the money.

(3) With intransitive verbs (of motion or action, which cannot be made passive as adjectives), the gerundive is used in the neuter, acting more like a noun. Again the agent is put in the dative.

> festinandum est nobis.
>
> *literally*   There is for us an act of hurrying needing to be done.
> *i.e.*   We must hurry.

Here the idea of necessity is expressed, but again English makes the meaning active rather than passive.

• Note that for all three gerundive jobs, Latin has other ways of saying the same thing. The adjective use and the instransitive neuter use could alternatively be expressed by *debeo* with the infinitive. The use with *ad* could alternatively be expressed by a purpose clause with *ut* (or *qui*) and the subjunctive (see pages 98 and 99).

• Deponent verbs (see page 69) have a gerundive of normal form which is passive in meaning.

Exercise 57   Gerundives

1   cibus in hortum portandus est.
2   murus servis aedificandus erat.
3   nuntius venerat ad verba regis narranda.
4   hi libri in flumen iniciendi sunt.
5   nautis ad insulam navigandum erat.
6   ille servus tibi fideliter custodiendus est.
7   nobis prope mare pugnandum erit.
8   epistula difficilis mihi scribenda est.
9   senex ad tabernam ambulabat ad cibum emendum.
10   tibi nunc est fugiendum.

Indirect statement

A statement is an ordinary sentence which is not a question or command. A *direct* statement may be the actual quoted words of a speaker:

> The messenger said 'The Romans have captured the city'.

Or it may be simply something the narrator tells us:

> After a long siege the Romans captured the city.

An *indirect* statement *reports* someone's words or thoughts (hence it is also called a *reported* statement):

> The messenger said that the Romans had captured the city.

> This historian claims that after a long siege the Romans captured the city.

English inserts the word *that* (though it can be omitted), then in effect starts a new sentence with its own subject and verb. Latin does it in a different way: the subject of the indirect statement becomes *accusative*, and the verb becomes *infinitive*. Hence this construction is commonly referred to as *accusative and infinitive*.

An accusative and infinitive is possible in English with some verbs:

> I believe the story to be true.

This sentence reports my original thought *The story is true*.

> The judge declared the winner to be this girl.

This sentence reports his original statement *The winner is this girl*. It may seem strange that a subject should be accusative, but imagine these sentences cut short: in *I believe the story* or *The judge declared the winner* it should be obvious that *story* and *winner* cannot be nominative.

• In these examples *I* and *judge* are nominative: a sentence can only introduce a *second* nominative if it has a second *finite* verb, with a person ending (see pages 2 and 46: the *infinitive* as its name implies is not finite).

In English the accusative and infinitive is not found very often, but in Latin it is used for *all* indirect statements. It is one of the most common of all constructions, and failure to recognise it is one of the main sources of confusion and error in GCSE.

Because this construction is used to report original direct statements which might have verbs in any tense, Latin needs to use a range of infinitives. See page 50 for the present active infinitive:

1st	portare	to carry
2nd	monere	to warn
3rd	trahere	to drag
4th	audire	to hear

See page 68 for the present passive infinitive:

1st	portari	to be carried
2nd	moneri	to be warned
3rd	trahi	to be dragged
4th	audiri	to be heard

These present infinitives are common in various contexts. Other infinitives are found mainly in indirect statements.

More infinitives

The *perfect active infinitive* (literally *to have X-ed*) is formed from the *perfect stem* (see page 54) plus *-isse*:

1st	portavisse	to have carried
2nd	monuisse	to have warned
3rd	traxisse	to have dragged
4th	audivisse	to have heard

The *perfect passive infinitive* (literally *to have been X-ed*) is formed from the *perfect passive participle* (see page 82) with the infinitive of the verb *to be* (see page 51):

1st	portatum* esse	to have been carried
2nd	monitum* esse	to have been warned
3rd	tractum* esse	to have been dragged
4th	auditum* esse	to have been heard

The future active infinitive (literally *to be going to X*) is formed from the future active participle (see page 86), again with the infinitive of the verb *to be* (see page 51):

1st	portaturum* esse	to be going to carry
2nd	moniturum* esse	to be going to warn
3rd	tracturum* esse	to be going to drag
4th	auditurum* esse	to be going to hear

* The participle is naturally accusative in indirect statement, but can be any gender, singular or plural (according to normal 2-1-2 endings: see page 16), agreeing with the subject of the infinitive. In the accusative and infinitive construction, the possibilities are as follows (using the perfect passive infinitive of *porto* as an example, but the pattern of endings applies to all perfect passive and future active infinitive):

	m	*f*	*n*
sg	portatum esse	portatam esse	portatum esse
pl	portatos esse	portatas esse	portata esse

Indirect statement

Indirect statements are most obviously introduced by verbs meaning *say*, *announce*, etc. But this construction is used also with verbs such as *think* and *know*: any verb that expresses the use of words, intellect, or the senses. Look out for it after the following:

dico	I say
narro	I tell
nuntio	I announce
respondeo	I reply
promitto	I promise
audio	I hear
video	I see
cognosco	I find out
intellego	I understand
scio	I know
credo	I believe
sentio	I feel

The tense of the infinitive is that of the original direct statement (the words of a speaker, or the implied statement representing someone's thoughts). To translate correctly you need to go through a two-stage process: thinking what the Latin says literally, then how this comes out in English.

If the introductory verb (the verb of *saying* etc, which is the main verb of the sentence, and can come anywhere within it) is present tense, this is straightforward:

	nuntius dicit navem appropinquare.
literally	The messenger says the ship to be approaching.
i.e.	The messenger says that the ship is approaching.

	audio hostes fugisse.
literally	I hear the enemy to have fled.
i.e.	I hear that the enemy have fled.

	credo has ancillas bene laboraturas esse.
literally	I believe these slave-girls to be going to work well.
i.e.	I believe that these slave-girls will work well.

Exercise 58   Indirect statement (with present tense main verb)

1   nuntius dicit homines crudeles ibi habitare.
2   video magnam turbam in forum convenire.
3   hic miles nuntiat urbem hostium captam esse.
4   audio omnes eos servos a domino custodiri.
5   nonne credis milites nostros fortiter pugnaturos esse?

Indirect statement

If the introductory verb is past tense (as it much more commonly is), the infinitive still has the tense of what was originally said or thought, but an adjustment has to be made in translation. This happens in English too: the direct statement *The ship is approaching* is reported afterwards as *The messenger said that the ship was approaching*. So if the introductory verb is in any past tense, the infinitive *moves a tense back* in translation:

> a present infinitive is translated as an imperfect tense
> a perfect infinitive is translated as a pluperfect tense
> a future infinitive is translated as a 'future in the past' (*was/were going to*)

Again the secret is to think first what the Latin says literally, then recast this as natural English.

> nuntius dixit navem appropinquare.
> *literally*   The messenger said the ship to be approaching.
> *i.e.*   The messenger said that the ship *was* approaching.

> audivi hostes fugisse.
> *literally*   I heard the enemy to have fled.
> *i.e.*   I heard that the enemy *had* fled.

> credebam has ancillas bene laboraturas esse.
> *literally*   I believed these slave-girls to be going to work well.
> *i.e,*   I believed that these slave-girls *were going to* (or *would*) work well.

The accusative subject must always be there in this construction, and indeed is one way of recognising it. If the subject of the infinitive is the same as the subject of the introductory verb, a reflexive pronoun is used, usually *se* (see page 27):

> nuntius dixit se quam celerrime cucurrisse.
> The messenger said that he had run as quickly as possible.

If *he* had referred to someone else, i.e. had not been reflexive, *eum* (see page 28) would have been used instead:

> femina, quae servum amabat, dixit eum bene laboravisse.
> The woman, who liked the slave, said that he had worked well

Because the infinitive has an accusative subject and may also have a direct object, two different accusatives may come one after the other. In such a sentence the first accusative will be the subject, the second one the object:

> credo senem pueros laudavisse.
> I believe that the old man praised the boys.

• Indirect statement can continue with another infinitive after a semi-colon (representing an original direct statement consisting of more than a single sentence):

> nuntius dixit bellum confectum esse; hostes fugisse; se haec a rege ipso audivisse.
> The messenger said that the war was finished, that the enemy had fled, and that he had heard these things from the king himself.

• A passive version of the indirect statement can be used. In this case the subject is nominative:

> servus dicitur stultus esse.
> The slave is said to be stupid.

If a perfect passive or future active infinitive is used like this, the participle forming part of it will be nominative:

> epistula dicitur missa esse.
> The letter is said to have been sent.

• Deponent and semi-deponent verbs (see pages 69-70) have a perfect active infinitive with the form of a perfect passive one, and a future active infinitive of the normal type.

> credo aliquem me secutum esse.
> I believe that someone followed me.

Exercise 59   Indirect statement (with past tense main verb)

1   miles nuntiavit hostes fugere.
2   cives audiverunt hostes fugisse.
3   puer dixit fratrem suum tandem dormire.
4   patrem meum fortissimum esse intellexi.
5   puella dixit se donum tuum amare.
6   mercator dixit se multam pecuniam in via amisisse.
7   scivistine illam domum venditam esse?
8   rex nesciebat omnes amicos fugisse.
9   senator dixit servum multos cives necavisse.
10   heri credidi nos in magno periculo futuros esse.

Exercise 60   Indirect statement (assorted tenses)

1   amicos discessuros esse forte cognovimus.
2   puellasne omnes adesse vides?
3   rex promisit se auxilium nobis missurum esse.
4   audio muros deletos esse.
5   femina dixit se sine marito iter fecisse.
6   spero patrem pecuniam mihi missurum esse.
7   nuntius narravit milites nostros multa mala passos esse.
8   aliquem appropinquare sensi.
9   novum templum aedificari video.
10   senex dixit se nihil audivisse; uxorem perterritam fuisse; domum incensam esse.

Imperfect subjunctive

The term *subjunctive* is not very informative: it means *joined under*, i.e. *bolted on*, as an alternative form of the verb, but without giving any clue about its use. It is basically a form of the verb which expresses a *possibility* rather than a fact (something that *might* happen, or *might* be the reason for something else).

The normal form in contrast is called *indicative* because it does state or *indicate* a fact (all ordinary verb forms with a tense and a person ending are indicative, though they are usually only described as such when they are being contrasted with the subjunctive).

The translation of the imperfect subjunctive varies according to the construction it is in.

It is very easy to form and recognise. The basic person endings (*-m, -s, -t, -mus, -tis, -nt*: see page 46) are stuck onto the infinitive.

sg	*1*	portare-m	monere-m	trahere-m	audire-m
	2	portare-s	monere-s	trahere-s	audire-s
	3	portare-t	*etc*	*etc*	*etc*
pl	*1*	portare-mus			
	2	portare-tis			
	3	portare-nt			

This also works for irregular verbs (see pages 51-2 and 60-2):

infinitive	*imperfect subjunctive*
esse	essem -es -et *etc*
posse	possem
ire	irem
velle	vellem
nolle	nollem
malle	mallem

The passive form of the imperfect subjunctive is made by changing the active endings to passive ones in the usual way (see page 64):

sg	*1*	portare-r	monere-r	trahere-r	audire-r
	2	portare-ris	monere-ris	trahere-ris	audire-ris
	3	portare-tur	*etc*	*etc*	*etc*
pl	*1*	portare-mur			
	2	portare-mini			
	3	portare-ntur			

Purpose clauses

One of the most common uses of the imperfect subjunctive is in a purpose clause, explaining the aim with which something was done.

> I went to Rome to see the emperor.
>
> He worked hard in order to get an A*.

Latin does not use the infinitive for this as you might expect from English, but instead uses the word *ut* (= in order to) with the imperfect subjunctive.

Translation as an infinitive in English often works if the subject of the purpose clause is the same as the subject of the main verb of the sentence:

> senex ad urbem ambulavit ut librum emeret.
>
> *literally*   The old man walked to the city in order that he might buy a book.
>
> *i.e.*   The old man walked to the city to buy a book.

If the purpose clause has a new subject, a translation such as *in order that* or *so that* is needed, putting *might* or *could* with the verb:

> femina totum diem laborabat ut liberi cibum haberent.
>
> The woman was working all day so that her children could have food.

A negative purpose clause uses *ne* (= in order not to) instead of *ut*:

> noctem exspectavimus ne ab hostibus videremur.
>
> We waited for night in order not to be seen by the enemy.

• A purpose clause is sometimes called a *final* clause, not because it comes last thing in the sentence (though it often does) but because it tells us the *end* in view, in the old sense of *aim*. For the use of *qui* (instead of *ut*) with the imperfect subjunctive to express purpose see page 99, and for the use of *ad* and the gerundive as a different way of expressing purpose see page 91.

• A purpose clause needs to be carefully distinguished from a result clause (also using *ut* and the imperfect subjunctive) which stresses the outcome rather than the intention: see page 102.

• The construction for a purpose clause is the same as for an indirect command (see page 100), and a negative purpose clause is also the same as the construction with a verb of fearing (see page 104).

• Note that *ut* with an ordinary indicative verb (or no verb at all) means *as*.

Exercise 61   Purpose clauses

1	pueri in via manere volebant ut puellas spectarent.
2	Romam ire constitui ut fratrem meum viderem.
3	femina clamavit ut ab omnibus audiretur.
4	servi diu laborabant ut novos muros aedificarent.
5	in taberna manebam ne verba imperatoris audirem.

(continued ...)

6	rex illos custodes habuit ne ab hostibus necaretur.
7	amici fideles advenerunt ut nos adiuvarent.
8	senex pecuniam in terra celavit ne uxor inveniret.
9	hi mortui sunt ut nos viveremus.
10	vos docebamini ut alios doceretis.

Use of *qui* for purpose

The relative pronoun *qui, quae, quod* (= who, which: see page 35) is often used with the imperfect subjunctive instead of *ut* to express purpose. This must be carefully distinguished from an ordinary relative clause, telling us a *fact* about the person or thing mentioned.

(1) *ordinary relative clause with an indicative verb:*

> misit nuntios qui regem necaverunt.
> He sent messengers who killed the king.

This tells us they were the people who went ahead and did it.

(2) qui *with the imperfect subjunctive expressing purpose:*

> misit nuntios qui regem necarent.
> He sent messengers to kill the king.

This tells us the intention in sending them, but not whether they actually did it.

• This second example could also be analysed as *who were to kill the king*, or *who could kill the king* (showing again how the subjunctive refers to a *possibility* rather than a fact, and also showing its flexibility), but it should be translated like a normal purpose clause.

• The relative pronoun in this construction is very often nominative, but not necessarily. As in a relative clause, it agrees with its antecedent in number and gender, but takes its case from the job it does in its own clause (see page 35):

> miles gladium ferebat quo se defenderet.
> The soldier was carrying a sword with which to defend himself.

• For another specialised use of the relative pronoun, as a *connecting relative*, see page 79.

Exercise 62   Use of *qui* for purpose

1	milites misi qui ducem hostium necarent.
2	senator servum qui equos suos curaret emit.
3	ancillas petere constitui quae in villa mea laborarent.
4	senex servum habebat qui pueros scelestos terreret.
5	imperatorem tandem invenimus qui hostes vinceret.

Indirect commands

For direct commands using the imperative see page 71. An *indirect* command reports a command, usually one previously given (compare page 92 on indirect statements, and page 108 on indirect questions).

direct: Be quiet!
indirect: I told the children to be quiet.

The verb *iubeo* (= I order) uses the infinitive for an indirect command just as English does:

> senator cives audire iussit.
> The senator ordered to citizens to listen.

Most other verbs use a clause with *ut* and the imperfect subjunctive, just like a purpose clause (see page 98). Note that *impero* (also = I order) takes a dative, because the idea is of giving an order *to* someone:

> senator civibus imperavit ut audirent.
> The senator ordered the citizens to listen.

• The construction is the same as for a purpose clause, because the underlying thought is the same. There is almost a pun on the word *order* in English: the senator gave an *order* to the citizens in *order* that they might listen, *i.e.* to achieve that purpose. Sometimes it is hard to tell the difference:

> epistulam amico scripsi ut in montes effugeret.

This could be read as a purpose clause:

> I wrote a letter to my friend so that he would escape into the mountains

Or as an indirect command:

> I wrote a letter to my friend telling him to escape into the mountains.

Nonetheless the two constructions are in practice classed separately.

A *command* in the grammatical sense can be a polite request or suggestion, rather than an actual order. Thus indirect commands can be introduced by a wide range of verbs, for example:

hortor	I encourage, I urge
moneo	I warn, I advise
oro	I beg
persuadeo	I persuade (+ *dat*)
rogo	I ask

A negative indirect command uses *ne* instead of *ut*, just as a negative purpose clause does:

> feminas monui ne diutius in foro manerent.
> I advised the women not to stay in the forum any longer.

Exercise 63   Indirect commands

1   senator nautas in portu laborare iussit.
2   dominus servo imperavit ut cibum in hortum portaret.
3   senex pueros ne trans viam ambularent monuit.
4   ancilla a patre meo iussa est cenam optimam parare.
5   civibus persuadere volui ne talia verba audirent.
6   imperator militibus imperavit ut per terram hostium lente progrederentur.
7   dux milites hortabatur ut ferocius pugnarent.
8   a principe rogatus eram ut in villa eius paucos dies manerem.
9   nonne a domino saepe monebaris ne in templo curreres?
10   rex omnes fugientes revocari iussit.

Exercise 64   Purpose clauses and indirect commands (revision)

1   matrem meam rogavi ut pecuniam mihi daret.
2   dux milites misit ut castra hostium invenirent.
3   imperator suis imperavit ut statim progrederentur.
4   multos dies in castris manebamus ne ab hostibus videremur.
5   senator cives hortabatur ut verbis suis crederent.
6   senex nos monebat ne prope flumen villam aedificaremus.
7   prima luce profecti sumus ut ante noctem adveniremus.
8   puer in montes fugit ne a patre inveniretur.
9   haec verba vobis locutus sum ut totam rem intellegeretis.
10   puellae ut de his rebus scriberet persuadere conatus sum.

Result clauses

A result clause focuses on the outcome of an action:

> He ran so fast that he won the prize.

It is recognised by a signpost word (*so* etc) in the first half of the sentence, then *ut* for *that* introducing the second half (the actual result clause), with the verb in the imperfect subjunctive to describe a result in the past.

The most common signpost words are:

tam	so	(*with an adjective or adverb*)
adeo	so much, to such an extent	(*with a verb*)

> haec puella tam fortis erat ut omnes eam laudarent.
> This girl was so brave that everyone praised her.

Note also some more specialised signpost words:

tantus	so big	(*used instead of* tam magnus)
tot	so many	(*used instead of* tam multi)
talis	such, of such a sort	

• Of these, *tantus* is normal 2-1-2 in declension (see page 16) and *talis* is a third declension adjective like *fortis* (see page 17); *tot* is indeclinable.

• Note the distinction between *tot* and the plural of *tantus*:

tot equi	so many horses
tanti equi	such big horses

• Note the similarity of these signpost words beginning *t-* to the question words beginning *qu-* (see page 73), which they can also be used to answer:

question		*answer*	
quantus	how big?	tantus	so big
quot	how many?	tot	so many
qualis	what sort?	talis	of such a sort, this sort

• Because a result clause depends so importantly on the signpost word in the first half, it is sometimes also called a *consecutive* (= following on) clause.

Result clauses

A result clause must be carefully distinguished from a purpose clause (which also uses *ut* and the subjunctive: see pages 98 and 113). It has a different emphasis:

(1) *purpose clause:*

> The boy worked hard in order to get an A*.

> That was the aim, but might not be the result: he could have been unlucky, or not worked quite hard enough.

(2) *result clause:*

> The boy worked so hard that he got an A*.

> That was the result, but might not have been the aim: he could have been unduly modest and aiming only for a B.

A purpose clause and a result clause both normally use *ut* and (in the examples you will meet in GCSE) the imperfect subjunctive. But if the clause contains a negative, there is an important difference: a negative purpose clause uses *ne* instead of *ut*, but a negative result clause uses *non* <u>as well as</u> *ut* (this is the only place where *ut* and *non* are used together).

> cibus talis erat ut eum edere non possem.
> The food was such (*or* so bad) that I could not eat it.

Note here that flexibility is needed in translation of *talis* according to context.

• On the use of negatives in general see page 110, and on the different uses of *ut* see page 113.

Exercise 65 Result clauses

1   dominus tam saevus erat ut omnes servi timerent.
2   ancilla tam bene laborabat ut ab omnibus laudaretur.
3   tanta erat turba ut non progredi possemus.
4   adeo terrebamur ut nihil faceremus.
5   equus talis erat ut nemo tenere posset.
6   nuntius tam celeriter locutus est ut verba eius iterum audire cogeremur.
7   tot epistulas acceperam ut non possem omnibus respondere.
8   miles adeo vulneratus erat ut mox moreretur.
9   tanti erant custodes ut nemo portam intrare vellet.
10   puer tam stultus erat ut nihil intellegeret.

Verbs of fearing

Verbs of fearing (*timeo*, and from the additional vocabulary the deponent verb *vereor*) can take a direct object or an infinitive, as in English:

> omnes nautae periculum maris timebant.
> All the sailors feared the danger of the sea.

> cur templum intrare times?
> Why are you afraid to enter the temple?

They also commonly take a clause using *ne* and the imperfect subjunctive, expressing what someone feared might happen. In form this construction is like a negative purpose clause (or indirect command) but is not negative in English. The old-fashioned word *lest* gives the sense exactly, but because it is no longer in common use is better avoided: modern English just says *that*.

> diu timebamus ne urbs nostra caperetur.
> We feared for a long time that our city would be captured.

• The reason a negative was used in the first place (though not translated as such) is that fearing is thought of as *hoping that something would not* happen.

• Note that *timeo* means *I fear*; *terreo* means *I frighten (someone)*. The English *I am frightened* (describing a state of mind) would be normally be represented in Latin by *timeo*. Note however that *perterritus* (the perfect passive participle of the compound *perterreo*, literally *I frighten thoroughly*) is used as an adjective meaning *terrified*.

• Note from the additional vocabulary the deponent verb *vereor* (= I fear, I am afraid). Its perfect active participle *veritus* (regular 2-1-2) is usually translated *fearing*, like a present participle.

It is also possible (though much less common) to express a negative fear, that something might *not* happen (i.e. you *hope it will* happen). For this Latin uses *ne* followed by *non*: the only place where *ne* and *non* are found together.

> timebam ne custos clamores non audiret.
> I feared that the guard might not hear the shouts.

Exercise 66   Verbs of fearing

1   timebam ne hostes advenirent.
2   timui e castris egredi.
3   puer ne inveniretur timebat.
4   timebamus ne imperator nos videret.
5   timuistine ne praemium non acciperes?

Time clauses with imperfect subjunctive

Time clauses, expressing when something happens, normally have an ordinary indicative verb in the same tense as the equivalent English, except that *dum* (= while) always has a present tense verb (see page 76). But *dum* can also be used with an imperfect subjunctive to mean *until*, and *priusquam* (= before) is used with an imperfect subjunctive if it means *before* something *could* or *got a chance to* happen: again, the subjunctive here expresses a possibility rather than a fact.

> cives in foro manebant dum senator adveniret.
> The citizens waited in the forum until the senator arrived (*or* could arrive).
> *or* The citizens waited in the forum for the senator to arrive.

This is in effect another form of disguised purpose clause (see pages 98-9): they waited *so that he could* arrive with them still there (he may or may not actually have done so).

> servus fugit priusquam dominus regrederetur.
> The slave ran away before his master returned (*or* could return).

This is similarly equivalent to a negative purpose clause: he escaped *so that his master would not* return to find him still there. It is also similar in thought to the construction with a verb of fearing (see page 104): he escaped *for fear that* his master would return. Note that this subjunctive construction with *priusquam* does not tell you whether or not the master did in fact afterwards return.

Contrast the ordinary use of *priusquam* with the indicative:

> priusquam hunc librum inveni, nihil intellegebam
> Before I found this book, I understood nothing.

• Compare the similarly contrasted uses of *qui, quae, quod* with an indicative verb for a relative clause (see page 35) and with an imperfect subjunctive for purpose (see page 99).

Exercise 67   Time clauses with subjunctive (*dum, priusquam*)

1   puer e villa cucurrit priusquam pater rediret.
2   Romae manebamus dum imperatorem videremus.
3   omnes discesserunt priusquam advenirem.
4   nuntium statim e foro misimus priusquam civibus totam rem narraret.
5   puellam manere iussi dum epistulam meam acciperet.

Pluperfect subjunctive

This is the second most common tense of the subjunctive after the imperfect, and the only other one needed for GCSE. The *imperfect* subjunctive is formed by adding the basic person endings (see page 46) to the *present* infinitive (see pages 50 and 97). By a similar process the pluperfect subjunctive is formed by adding the same basic person endings to the *perfect* infinitive (see page 93), again producing a tense one back from the infinitive involved.

The imperfect subjunctive cannot be translated in isolation because it depends on its job in a construction. The pluperfect subjunctive on the other hand translates just like a normal pluperfect. Expect to see it in two constructions described below: *cum* clauses (page 107) and indirect questions (page 108).

sg	*1*	portavisse-m	monuisse-m	traxisse-m	audivisse-m
	2	portavisse-s	monuiss-es	traxisse-s	audivisse-s
	3	portavisse-t	*etc*	*etc*	*etc*
pl	*1*	portavisse-mus			
	2	portavisse-tis			
	3	portavisse-nt			

Again this works also for irregular verbs (see pages 51-2 and 60-2), for example:

verb	*perfect tense*	*perfect infinitive*	*pluperfect subjunctive*
sum	fui	fuisse	fuissem
possum	potui	potuisse	potuissem
eo	i(v)i	iisse	i(v)issem
volo	volui	voluisse	voluissem
nolo	nolui	noluisse	noluissem
malo	malui	maluisse	maluissem

The passive form of the pluperfect subjunctive simply takes the ordinary pluperfect passive (see page 67) and puts the auxiliary verb, which is the imperfect of *to be*, into its subjunctive form (see page 97):

sg	*1*	portatus essem
	2	portatus esses
	3	portatus esset
pl	*1*	portati essemus
	2	portati essetis
	3	portati essent

As with the ordinary pluperfect passive (see page 67), the perfect passive participle (see page 82) forming the first part of this tense agrees in number and gender with the subject of the sentence.

Similarly for the other conjugations: *monitus essem, tractus essem, auditus essem.*

Cum clauses

Clauses telling us *when* or *why* something happened commonly have a word such as *ubi* (= when) or *quod* (= because) with an ordinary indicative verb (see pages 76 and 77).

> ubi Romam adveneram, de morte imperatoris audivi.
> When I had arrived in Rome, I heard about the death of the emperor.

> servus, quod dormiebat, nihil audivit.
> The slave, because he was asleep, heard nothing.

The first example states that two things happened one after the other. The second tells us one thing that is definitely the reason for the other. Indicative verbs (see page 97) are appropriate because facts are being stated.

In either of these sentences *cum* (translated *when* or *since*) with the appropriate tense of the subjunctive could have been used instead:

> cum Romam advenissem, de morte imperatoris audivi.
> servus, cum dormiret, nihil audivit.

In practice the meaning would be virtually the same as in the previous versions. The slight difference of emphasis is to convey a *suggested reason*: it was *only* by arriving then that I heard the news (and so not just a coincidence of time); it was *presumably* because the slave was asleep (rather than that he was stone deaf or very drunk).

Cum clauses are very common. The imperfect or pluperfect subjunctive translates according to sense, coming out as the same tense in English. The word *since* is favoured because it suggests 'a *when* that is also a *because*'. (This use of *since* in English must be distinguished from its other sense *from the time when*.)

• Note that this *cum* is a completely separate word from the preposition *cum* used with the ablative and meaning *with* (see pages 42 and 113): these are *homonyms*.

Exercise 68   *Cum* clauses

1   cives, cum hostes urbi appropinquarent, perterriti erant.
2   senex, cum ad forum ambularet, multam pecuniam invenit.
3   illis hominibus non credidi cum stulti essent.
4   laeti eramus cum consilium novum intellexissemus.
5   cum omnes feminae advenissent, a viris salutatae sunt.
6   rex, cum iam discedere constituisset, hoc statim fecit.
7   cum montem ascenderem vulnus severum accepi.
8   dominus, cum totam rem audivisset, servum fidelem laudavit.
9   liberi gaudebant cum nihil scribere deberent.
10   nonne iratus eras cum murum deletum conspexisses?

Indirect questions

This construction reports a direct question (see pages 72-3) previously asked, just as an indirect statement reports a statement (see pages 92-6) and an indirect command reports a command (see page 100):

direct: Why are you silent?
indirect: I asked the slave why he was silent.

Here Latin moves a tense back in changing from the direct to the reported form, just like English does (contrast indirect statement, where the infinitive retains the tense of the original direct statement). The verb in the indirect question is imperfect or pluperfect subjunctive: a present tense in the direct question comes out as an imperfect, a past tense as a pluperfect. Each translates naturally into English.

direct: cur taces?
Why are you silent?

indirect: servum rogavi cur taceret.
I asked the slave why he was silent.

direct: quis epistulam scripsit?
Who wrote the letter?

indirect: senex filiam rogavit quis epistulam scripsisset.
The old man asked his daughter who had written the letter.

All the question words asking for specific information (e.g. *why, who, what, when, where, how*: see page 73) are used in indirect questions just as in direct ones.

With questions asking if something is the case (to which the answer will be *Yes* or *No*), there is a very important difference. *Direct* questions (see page 72) can be slanted according to the answer the questioner hopes for:

-ne (*added to first word*) is it the case? (*open*)
nonne   surely ... ?   (*hoping for the answer* Yes)
num   surely ... not? (*hoping for the answer* No)

In an *indirect* question this distinction cannot be shown, and any question to which the answer will be *Yes* or *No* is introduced by *num*, here meaning *whether*. Note therefore the important rule (see also page 113):

| num | in a <u>direct</u> question | surely not? |
| | in an <u>indirect</u> question | whether |

senem rogavi num fratrem meum vidisset.
I asked the old man whether he had seen my brother.

The original direct question reported here might have been a *-ne, nonne,* or *num* type: all come out the same in the indirect form.

Indirect questions

• Note that *if* is another possible translation of *num* in an indirect question, but it should not be confused with *si* (= if) which is used only in a conditional clause (see page 78).

An indirect question posing two alternatives uses *utrum ... an* (whether ... or):

> femina servum rogavit utrum malus an stultus esset.
> The woman asked the slave whether he was evil or stupid.

An indirect question is often used when the original direct question is only implied:

> difficile erat nobis cognoscere quid accidisset.
> It was difficult for us to find out what had happened.

Here the direct question *What happened?* might have existed only in our minds. A verb suggesting *asking* need not be involved at all:

> puer nuntiavit quid fecisset.
> The boy reported what he had done.

Here the idea is that he said *what it was* that he had done, again answering an implied question *What did you do?* An indirect question can be harder to spot than some constructions, but in practice this does not matter because it usually translates naturally into English.

• Note the difference between an indirect question and a relative clause (see page 35-6):

(1) *indirect question*

> puellam rogavi quem ibi vidisset.
> I asked the girl whom she had seen there.

(2) *relative clause*

> puella nihil dicere poterat de homine quem ibi viderat.
> The girl could say nothing about the man whom she had seen there.

Exercise 69   Indirect questions

1   pueros rogavi num seni adiuvare conati essent.
2   nemo scivit quid agerem.
3   volo cognoscere ubi heri esses.
4   mater me iterum quid facerem rogavit.
5   imperator cognoscere voluit quis naves hostium vidisset.
6   intellegere non poteram quid ibi faceretur.
7   dominus quo modo omnes servi fugissent nesciebat.
8   filium meum rogavi utrum manere an abire vellet.
9   cives tandem audiverunt quid a rege dictum esset.
10   servum rogavi utrum cibum an vinum cepisset.

Negatives

The normal negative is *non* and its normal position is just in front of the verb:

> aquam non amo.
> I do not like water.

If *non* is put elsewhere in the sentence, it negatives the word it is just in front of:

> non aquam sed vinum amo.
> I like not water but wine.

Note the paired negatives *nec ... nec* (or *neque ... neque*) = neither ... nor:

> neque aquam neque vinum amo.
> I like neither water nor wine.
> *or*　I do not like either water or wine.

• Note that *numquam* (= never) is the negative of *umquam* (= ever).

• From the additional vocabulary list note *haud*, a negative commonly used with adverbs:

> pater meus haud saepe talia dicit.
> My father does not often say such things.

The negative for a possibility rather than a fact is *ne*. This is used (instead of *ut*) for a negative purpose clause (see page 98):

> servus e villa cucurrit ne a domino videretur.
> The slave ran out of the house in order not to be seen by his master.

Exactly the same construction is used for a negative indirect command (see page 100):

> senex pueris imperavit ne in templo clamarent.
> The old man ordered the boys not to shout in the temple.

Other subjunctive constructions, i.e. result clause (page 103), *cum* clause (page 107), and indirect question (page 108) use the normal negative *non*.

No as the opposite of *Yes* is *minime* (adverb of *minimus*, also used in its literal sense *very little*, *least*). *No* as an adjective meaning *not any* is *nullus*. For the pronouns *nemo* (= no-one) and *nihil* (= nothing), see page 40.

• From the additional vocabulary note the plural adjective *nonnulli -ae -a* = some, several (literally a double negative *not no*).

• Note that *ne* is also used after a verb of fearing, but is not translated as a negative: see page 104.

• For negative direct commands using *noli* (plural *nolite*) see page 71.

• For the direct question words *nonne* (= surely?) and *num* (= surely not?) see page 72.

Translating complex sentences

Latin typically tells a story not in a series of short sentences (or clauses equivalent to separate sentences, joined by *and* or *but*); it prefers instead more complex sentences with one *main* clause (which could stand alone) and one or more *subordinate* clauses (which would not make sense in isolation). Here are some typical examples of subordinate clauses:

(1) When we had arrived in Rome ...   (5) ... whom I saw yesterday
(2) ... to find the book   (6) Although I had heard nothing ...
(3) If you give me the money ...   (7) ... that she understood everything
(4) ... in order to guard the walls   (8) ... who had sent the letter

Try identifying which type of clause each one is (some could be more than one). Many of the constructions described in this book count as subordinate clauses.

To find your way through a difficult sentence, try to find the main clause; bracket off (mentally or on paper) the subordinate bit or bits, then decide how to put the whole thing together. Thought needs to be given to appropriate expression in English.

> Romani, postquam in castra advenerunt, cibum postulaverunt.
> *literally*   The Romans, after they arrived in the camp, demanded food.

A very common mistake in GCSE is to write:

> The Romans, after they arrived in the camp, they demanded food.

This is wrong because it puts in too many subjects (*The Romans ... they ... they*). There are two verbs, and two clauses, so there can only be two subjects. But the candidate who made this mistake sensed rightly that the literal translation sounds awkward. The best solution here is to put *the Romans* inside the subordinate clause:

> After the Romans arrived in the camp, they demanded food.

A participle often needs to be translated as subordinate clause: see pages 81, 83 and 86. A perfect passive participle can be translated as an active verb if it is clear from the context that the action has been done by the person who is subject of the sentence:

> puer puellam conspectam salutavit.
> *literally*   The boy greeted the having been caught sight of girl.
> *i.e.*   The boy greeted the girl he had caught sight of.

An ablative absolute (see pages 87-9) is often translated as a subordinate clause:

> his verbis dictis nuntius discessit.
> When he had said these words the messenger left.

But it is also acceptable to make two main clauses, joined by *and*: the clauses are now *co-ordinated* (i.e. both of equal importance):

> The messenger said these words and left.

111

Double subordination is when one subordinate clause has another clause (or an ablative absolute, or other participle phrase) inside it. It is usually better in English to make the two subordinate elements parallel to each other:

> milites misi qui rege interfecto urbem caperent.
> *literally* I sent soldiers in order that, with the king having been killed, they could capture the city.
> *i.e.* I sent soldiers to kill the king and capture the city.

Here the ablative absolute has been treated like another purpose clause.

> cum senator epistula lecta surrexisset, omnes tacuerunt.
> *literally* When the senator, with the letter having been read, had stood up, everyone was silent.
> *i.e.* When the senator had read the letter and stood up, everyone was silent.

Here the ablative absolute has been treated like another *cum* clause.

> deus dixit hunc hominem, Romam ingressum, regem futurum esse.
> *literally* The god said that this man, having entered Rome, would be king.
> *i.e.* The god said that this man would enter Rome and be king.

Here the participle phrase has been treated like another indirect statement.
Sometimes a double subordination can be retained in English:

> cum omnes qui audire volebant advenissent, senator loqui coepit.
> When everyone who wanted to listen had arrived, the senator began to speak.

Here the relative clause has been translated literally, inside the *cum* clause.

Exercise 70   Complex sentences

1   haec puella promittit se labore confecto ceteras adiuturam esse.
2   Romani, cum bellum eo loco gererent, montem ascenderunt ut castra hostium subito oppugnarent.
3   verbis nuntii auditis, magna turba civium in forum convenit ad senatorem redeuntem exspectandum.
4   ubi urbe capta muri deleti erant, omnes ad portum festinavimus.
5   multis post annis, dum Romae habito, feminam olim conspectam iterum petere constitui.
6   pueri qui in via aderant adeo clamaverunt ut timerem ne ab imperatore audirentur.
7   missis aliquibus qui portas custodirent, dux suis ut lente progrederentur imperavit.
8   postquam omnes epistulas a te scriptas legi, totam rem multo verius intellegebam.
9   servus qui vinum iam abstulerat deinde pecunia rapta e villa fugit priusquam a domino inveniretur.
10   ubi primum nomen huius regis audivi, sensi eum fratre interfecto crudeliorem futurum esse.

Important words with more than one meaning

Some of these are alternative meanings of what is in origin the same word, others are homonyms (unrelated words which are coincidentally spelled in the same way).

				see page:
ad	(1)	to, towards, at	preposition with the accusative	41
	(2)	in order to	followed by gerundive	91
cum	(1)	with	preposition with the ablative	42
	(2)	when, since	introducing clause with subjunctive verb	107
hic	(1)	this	masculine nominative singular pronoun	31
	(2)	here	adverb	23
ne	(1)	not, not to	negative in purpose clause	98
			or indirect command	100
	(2)	that	after verb of fearing	104
(-ne)	(3)	is it (etc)?	signals a question, attached to its first word	72
num	(1)	surely not?	in direct question	72
	(2)	whether	in indirect question	108
quam	(1)	how	in direct question or exclamation	73
	(2)	than	in comparison	19
	(3)	... as possible	with superlative adverb	24
	(4)	whom, which	feminine accusative singular	
			of relative pronoun	35, 79
quod	(1)	because	introducing clause giving reason	77
	(2)	which	neuter nominative or accusative singular	
			of relative pronoun	35, 79
ubi	(1)	when	introducing a time clause	76
	(2)	where	introducing a question	73
			or a clause explaining location	76

Note: *ubi* as a question must be *where*, if not a question can be *when* or *where*.

ut	(1)	(in order) to	introducing a purpose clause	98
	(2)	to	introducing an indirect command	100
	(3)	that	introducing a result clause	102
	(4)	as	with indicative verb, or no verb	98

Exercise 71   Important words with more than one meaning (i)

1   servis imperavi ut celeriter laborarent.
2   servi celeriter laborabant ut laborem conficerent.
3   servi tam celeriter laborabant ut a domino saepe laudarentur.
4   servi, ut antea dixi, celeriter laborabant.
5   donum puellae misi quod tristissima erat.
6   donum quod puellae misi ei placuit.
7   senex fortior est quam iuvenis.
8   quam fortis es, amice!
9   quam graviter vulneratus est imperator?
10   ancilla quam heri vidi pulcherrima est.

Exercise 72   Important words with more than one meaning (ii)

1   milites tacebant ne ab hostibus invenirentur.
2   servis imperavi ne in horto clamarent.
3   cives timebant ne hostes urbem caperent.
4   tune haec scripsisti?
5   Romam cum fratre meo ire constitui.
6   cum frater meus domi manere mallet, Romam solus profectus sum.
7   servi, cum diu laboravissent, dormire volebant.
8   num illum librum legisti?
9   puerum rogavi num illum librum legisset.
10   puerone imperavisti ne illum librum legeret?

Words easily confused

Additional vocabulary only

absum	I am away	iaceo	I lie (down)
adsum	I am here	iacio	I throw
alter	one/the other (of two)	ita	in this way, so
altus	high, deep	itaque	and so, therefore
ante	before (*prep + acc*)	iter	journey
antea	before, previously	iterum	again
aperio	I open	laetus	happy
appareo	I appear	latus (i)	wide
		latus (ii)	having been carried
audeo*	I dare		
audio	I hear	liber	book
		liberi	children
carus	dear	libero	I set free
clarus*	famous	libertas*	freedom
		libertus	freedman, ex-slave
cogito	I think		
cognosco	I get to know	malo	I prefer
cogo	I force	malus	bad
curo	I look after	morbus*	illness
curro	I run	mors	death
		mos*	custom
dico	I say		
duco	I lead	novem	nine
		novus	new
domina	mistress		
dominus	master	parco*	I spare
domus	house	pareo*	I obey
		paro	I prepare
forte	by chance		
fortis	brave, strong	porta	gate
fortiter	bravely, strongly	porto	I carry
		portus	harbour
habeo	I have		
habito	I live	post	after (*prep + acc*)
		postea	afterwards
hortor	I encourage	postquam	after (*X happened, ...*)
hortus	garden		

115

reddo	I give back	summus	top (of)
redeo	I go back	sumus	we are
rideo	I laugh		
		tamen	however
res (*acc* rem)	thing	tandem	at last
rex (*acc* regem)	king		
		terreo	I frighten
saepe	often	timeo	I fear
semper	always		
		trado	I hand over
simul*	at the same time	traho	I drag
simulac	as soon as		
		vici	I conquered
soleo*	I am accustomed	vixi	I lived
solus	alone		
		vulnus	wound
stat	he stands	vultus	face
statim	at once, immediately		
subito	suddenly		

Exercise 73   Words easily confused (i)

1   pueros de verbis quae cognoverant cogitare coegi.
2   ego diu aberam; libertus tamen qui aderat libros liberis tandem dedit.
3   a domino domum missus sum.
4   pater nos ut in horto maneremus hortatus est.
5   hic puer semper redit, semper ridet; sed pecuniam saepe non reddit.
6   ego post portam iacebam, sed frater meus libros in portum postea iaciebat.
7   milites muros fortiter custodiebant sed ducem hostium forte non viderunt.
8   hic miles qui vulnus in vultu habet hic habitat.
9   summus mons ubi nunc sumus altior altero est.
10   malo omnia ipse trahere quam malo servo tradere.

Exercise 74   Words easily confused (ii) (including words from the additional vocabulary)

1   milites fideles ubi dico omnia audiunt, ubi duco omnia audent.
2   dei soli omnia scire solent.
3   filia cara dominae nostrae domum currebat ut equum clarum curaret.
4   mos est nobis de morbo regis tacere, sed mortem eius statim nuntiare.
5   senex senatori parebat, sed ei ut sibi parceret persuadere parabat.

Summary of uses of the subjunctive

• Expect to see an *imperfect* subjunctive (see page 97) in the following constructions:
purpose clause (see page 98)
> Romam ivimus ut imperatorem videremus.
> We went to Rome to see the emperor.

after qui *expressing purpose* (see page 99)
> milites misi qui murum delerent.
> I sent soldiers to destroy the wall.

indirect command (see page 100)
> dominus servis imperavit ut celerius laborarent.
> The master ordered the slaves to work more quickly.

result clause (see page 102)
> puer tam stultus erat ut nihil intellegeret.
> The boy was so stupid that he understood nothing.

clause after verb of fearing (see page 104)
> cives timebant ne portus oppugnaretur.
> The citizens were afraid that the harbour would be attacked

time clause expressing a possibility (see page 105)
> omnem cibum consumpsi priusquam frater eum inveniret.
> I ate all the food before my brother could find it.

cum *clause* (see page 107)
> cum nullam pecuniam haberemus, miserrimi eramus.
> Since we had no money, we were very miserable.

indirect question (see page 108)
> puerum rogavi quid consumeret.
> I asked the boy what he was eating.

• Expect to see a *pluperfect* subjunctive (see page 106) in the following constructions:
cum *clause* (see page 107)
> cum nihil audivissem, domi manebam.
> Since I had heard nothing, I stayed at home.

indirect question (see page 108)
> puellam rogavi quid fecisset.
> I asked the girl what she had done.

Exercise 75   Uses of the subjunctive

1   pueri adeo clamabant ut verba mea audire non possent.
2   milites nostri semper fortiter pugnabant ut hostes vincerent.
3   pater filio imperavit ut statim rediret.
4   cives num hostes fugissent cognoscere conabantur.
5   cum via longissima esset, media nocte advenimus.
6   patri meo persuasi ut domum veniret.
7   dominus servos rogavit quid ibi facerent.
8   frater meus, cum tot praemia accepisset, laetissimus erat.
9   dux milites misit qui castra hostium invenirent.
10   servus in silva se celavit ne a domino crudeli inveniretur.

Practice passages for unseen translation

Passage 1

Damocles learns that the life of a tyrant is less enviable than he thought.

Dionysius erat tyrannus Syracusanorum. cives eum tyrannum fecerant quod hostes suos
vicerat. comes quidam Damocles nomine saepe loquebatur de imperio atque divitiis
tyranni, cuius vitam laetissimam esse credebat. itaque Dionysius 'visne igitur' inquit
'hanc vitam, quod tibi ita placet, ipse degustare?' cum Damocles dixisset se hoc cupere,
5   Dionysius eum ad cenam magnificam invitavit.

mensae cibo optimo gravissimae erant et vinum optimum liberaliter fundebatur. sed
super lectum ubi Damocles recumbebat Dionysius gladium ingentem posuerat ut capiti
eius impenderet. filum quod gladium tenebat tenuissimum erat. itaque Damocles,
veritus ne subito necaretur, per totam cenam gladium intente spectabat. adeo timebat ut
10   cibum consumere non posset, vinum bibere nollet. tyrannum igitur tandem oravit ut sibi
domum redire permitteret, cum vitam eius habere non iam nollet. intellexit enim
tyrannum nihil gaudii habere cum metus ei semper impenderet.

Names

Dionysius -i (*m*)	Dionysius
Syracusani -orum (*m pl*)	Syracusans, people of Syracuse (*a city in Sicily*)
Damocles -is (*m*)	Damocles

Vocabulary

tyrannus -i (*m*)	tyrant, ruler
divitiae -arum (*f pl*)	riches, wealth
degusto -are	I have a taste of
magnificus -a -um	magnificent
mensa -ae (*f*)	table
liberaliter	generously
lectus -i (*m*)	couch
recumbo -ere	I recline
impendo -ere	I hang over (+ *dat*)
filum -i (*n*)	thread
tenuis -e	thin
intente	intently

Passage 2

Alexander the Great comes to power and describes his military ambitions.

cum <u>Philippus</u> <u>Macedonum</u> rex ab inimico necatus esset, regnum <u>obtinuit</u> <u>Alexander</u>
filius eius, iuvenis tum <u>viginti</u> annos <u>natus</u>. hic statim in pericula maxima venit: gentes
enim a <u>Philippo</u> victae sperabant se <u>rebellione</u> facta libertatem suam facile <u>recuperaturas</u>
<u>esse</u>. <u>Alexander</u> autem tam celeriter in hostium terram profectus est ut nemo resistere
5   posset et omnes sine proelio eum victorem salutarent.

deinde <u>Alexander</u> ducibus <u>Graecorum</u> <u>convocatis</u> nuntiavit se in <u>Asiam</u> exercitum
magnum ducturum esse ut <u>Dario</u> e regno expulso locum eius ipse teneret. '<u>Achilles</u>
olim' inquit 'e gente mea miles fortissimus, in <u>Asia</u> <u>gloriam</u> bello accepit: cuius exemplo
ego in <u>Asiam</u> profectus hos <u>barbaros</u> puniam qui, tribus <u>incursionibus</u> in <u>Graeciam</u>
10   factis, <u>maioribus</u> nostris iniurias gravissimas fecerunt.' quae cum dixisset, <u>Graeci</u> magno
clamore sublato <u>Alexandrum</u> laudaverunt et se copias ei daturos esse promiserunt.

Names

Philippus -i (*m*)	Philip
Macedones -um (*m pl*)	Macedonians
Alexander -dri (*m*)	Alexander
Graecus -a -um	Greek
Asia -ae (*f*)	Asia
Darius -i (*m*)	Darius
Achilles -is (*m*)	Achilles
Graecia -ae (*f*)	Greece

Vocabulary

obtineo -ere -ui	I succeed to, I take over
viginti	twenty
natus -a -um	old, aged
rebellio -onis (*f*)	rebellion
recupero -are -avi -atus	I get (something) back
convoco -are -avi -atus	I call together
gloria -ae (*f*)	glory
barbari -orum (*m pl*)	barbarians
incursio -onis (*f*)	invasion
maiores -um (*m pl*)	ancestors

Passage 3

The philosopher and mathematician Archimedes is tragically killed.

Romani Syracusam primo navibus oppugnare conati sunt. deinde, quod urbem hoc modo capere non poterant, duos annos obsidebant. cives ubi tandem victi sunt nihil aliud quam salutem sibi liberisque rogaverunt; quae a Romanis promissa est. urbs tamen militibus data est ut praedam peterent. multa tum irae exempla erant, multa
5   avaritiae.

inter haec Archimedes philosophus interfectus est. nam inter tumultum urbis captae, miles Romanus domum quandam intravit ut aurum caperet. ibi hominem conspexit quem nesciebat. miles eum rogavit quis esset. philosophus tamen formas quas in pulvere scripserat inspiciebat. nihil dixit. Romanus igitur ei imperavit ut statim
10   responderet. sed Archimedes formis suis tam intentus erat ut verba militis non audiret. tum Romanus ira incensus nulla mora Graecum necavit. imperator tamen exercitus Romanorum, Marcellus nomine, quod mortem philosophi graviter tulit, militem severissime puniri iussit.

Names

Syracusa -ae (*f*)	Syracuse (*a city in Sicily*)
Archimedes -is (*m*)	Archimedes
Graecus -a -um	Greek
Marcellus -i (*m*)	Marcellus

Vocabulary

obsideo -ere	I besiege
salus -utis (*f*)	safety
praeda -ae (*f*)	spoil, plunder
avaritia -ae (*f*)	greed
philosophus -i (*m*)	philosopher
tumultus -us (*m*)	commotion, uproar
forma -ae (*f*)	shape, diagram
pulvis -eris (*m*)	dust
inspicio -ere	I look at, I examine
intentus -a -um	intent
mora -ae (*f*)	delay

Passage 4

King Tarquinius buys some unusual books.

anus incognita ad Tarquinium Superbum regem adiit. novem libros ferebat quos oracula
deorum esse dicebat. libros vendere volebat, sed tantam pecuniam postulavit ut rex
ridens anum insanam esse crederet. deinde illa ad focum ambulavit et tres libros in
ignem iniecit. his deletis, Tarquinium rogavit num libros reliquos eodem pretio emere
5 vellet. illi tamen non persuasit: rex multo magis risit. itaque anus tres alios libros statim
incendit. quod cum fecisset, placide rogavit num tres reliquos eodem pretio empturus
esset.

Tarquinius tandem, quod tantam constantiam non neglegendam esse intellexit, anui
paruit. libros igitur tres emit non minore pretio quam pro omnibus primo petitum erat. et
10 illa cum a rege discessisset postea numquam visa est. libri tres, in templo positi,
diligenter custodiebantur. consilium eorum semper petebatur ubi populus Romanus de
periculo liberandus erat.

Names

      Tarquinius -i Superbus -i (*m*)   Tarquinius Superbus (*also called just Tarquinius*)

Vocabulary

anus -us (*f*)	old woman
incognitus -a -um	unknown
oraculum -i (*n*)	oracle
insanus -a -um	insane, mad
focus -i (*m*)	hearth
reliquus -a -um	remaining
pretium -i (*n*)	price
placide	calmly
constantia -ae (*f*)	perseverance
neglego -ere	I disregard
populus -i (*m*)	people

Passage 5

Lucretia is shamefully treated but remains noble to the end.

Roma regebatur a rege superbo, cuius filius erat Sextus Tarquinius. quadam nocte cum
Tarquinius et amici vinum biberent, coeperunt uxores suas laudare. Collatinus dixit
suam Lucretiam optimam esse. 'quid creditis eam nunc facere?' inquit 'ego vos ad
villam meam ducam. tum videbitis eam meliorem esse ceteris.' hoc omnibus placuit.
5 cum ad villam advenissent, Lucretiam non ludentem sed lanam ducentem invenerunt.
Sextus tamen, cum videret quam pulchra Lucretia esset, amore scelesto captus est.

paucis post diebus, cum abesset Collatinus, ille regressus cubiculum Lucretiae intravit.
'tace' inquit 'Sextus Tarquinius sum. ferrum in manu fero. aut cede mihi aut te necabo!'
quamquam Lucretia dixit se necari malle, Sextus tandem pudicitiam eius vicit. tum
10 discessit. Collatinus, cum omnia audivisset, iuravit se Sextum puniturum esse. Lucretia,
ne aliis uxoribus malum exemplum esse videretur, se necavit. 'ego me non culpo, sed
poena non libero' moriens dixit.

Names

Sextus -i Tarquinius -i (*m*)	Sextus Tarquinius (*called by either or both names*)
Collatinus -i (*m*)	Collatinus
Lucretia -ae (*f*)	Lucretia

Vocabulary

superbus -a -um	proud, arrogant
ludo -ere	I play
lanam duco -ere	I spin wool
cubiculum -i (*n*)	bedroom
cedo -ere	I yield, I give way
pudicitia -ae (*f*)	modesty, virtue
iuro -are -avi	I swear

Passage 6

Horatius defends the single bridge over the Tiber from enemy attack.

nemo praeter duos comites, viros audaces, cum Horatio nunc manebat. ceteris pontem a
tergo ferro et igni delere iussis, periculum impetus cum his primo ferebat. deinde, cum
parva pars pontis maneret, comites in locum tutum abire coegit. Horatius, qui antea
promiserat se urbem servaturum esse, in ponte solus contra multos stabat. duces
5   hostium saevissime spectabat ut ad pugnam provocaret. tot hostes iam interfecerat ut
ceteri primo progredi timerent. sed tandem illi magno cum clamore tela in unum
Romanum iecerunt.

Horatius magna virtute se scuto defendebat. subito tamen, ponte tandem rupto,
clamorem suorum audivit. tum Horatius, multis vulneribus acceptis, deo fluminis
10   precatus est. 'Tiberine pater' inquit 'accipe hunc militem et haec arma flumine tuo.'
deinde in aquam desiluit armatus. quamquam multa tela ab hostibus iaciebantur, ad
alteram ripam tutus tranavit.

Names

Horatius -i (*m*)	Horatius
Tiberinus -i (*m*)	Tiberinus (*god of the Tiber*)

Vocabulary

pons pontis (*m*)	bridge
tergum -i (*n*)	back
tutus -a -um	safe
pugna -ae (*f*)	fight
provoco -are	I provoke, I challenge
telum -i (*n*)	weapon, missile
scutum -i (*n*)	shield
desilio -ire -ui	I jump down
armatus -a -um	fully armed
ripa -ae (*f*)	bank
trano -are -avi	I swim across

Passage 7

Menenius Agrippa gives advice by telling a story.

olim erat inter Romanos magna <u>discordia</u>. milites enim cum ducibus suis parere nollent
ex urbe in montem quendam discesserant. cives igitur perterriti <u>Menenium Agrippam</u>,
virum sapientem militibusque carum, ad eos reducendos miserunt. ille, ubi in montem
venit, <u>fabulam</u> eis narravit.

5 'olim erat in corpore magna <u>discordia</u>. partes enim corporis <u>ventrem</u> magno clamore
simul culpabant. omnes dixerunt <u>ventrem</u> cibum suo labore datum semper consumere
sed ipsum in medio sedentem nihil facere. itaque manus "cibum" inquit "ad <u>os</u> non
portabo". <u>os</u> dixit se cibum accipere nolle, <u>dentesque</u> "nos" inquiunt "cibum non
manducabimus". <u>venter</u> igitur cum cibum non haberet in magno periculo mox erat. non
10 tamen <u>ventrem</u> vicerunt partes corporis, sed ipsae in periculum mortis venerunt. nam
sanguinem, quem <u>venter</u> corpori praebet, sine auxilio eius non habuerunt.' <u>Menenius</u>
<u>Agrippa</u> igitur his verbis militibus persuasit ut in urbem regrederentur.

Names

      Menenius -i Agrippa -ae (*m*)   Menenius Agrippa (*also called just Agrippa*)

Vocabulary

      discordia -ae (*f*)   disagreement
      fabula -ae (*f*)   story
      venter -tris (*m*)   stomach
      os oris (*n*)   mouth
      dens dentis (*m*)   tooth
      manduco -are   I chew

Passage 8

Coriolanus is forced to change his mind about attacking his own city.

Coriolanus qui dux Romanorum fuerat a populo suo expulsus est. ab urbe fugit ad
Volscos qui illo tempore bellum contra Romanos gerebant. feminae igitur Romanae,
veritae ne Coriolanus patriam oppugnaret, ad matrem uxoremque eius venerunt. quibus
persuaserunt ut secum ad castra hostium adirent. feminae enim sperabant se urbem, cum
5   armis defendere non possent, precibus lacrimisque servaturas esse.

cum ad castra pervenissent amicus quidam Coriolano nuntiavit magnam turbam
feminarum adesse. ille primo quaerere noluit quid vellent. deinde amicus, qui illas
cognoverat, 'nisi oculi me decipiunt' inquit 'mater tua et uxor adsunt, cum duobus parvis
filiis.' tum Coriolanus surrexit ad eas salutandas. sed mater irata rogavit utrum ad filium
10 an ad hostem venisset, utrum captiva an mater in castris eius esset. quibus verbis
permotus Coriolanus exercitum ab urbe movit sed postea a Volscis interfectus est.

Names

| Coriolanus -i (*m*) | Coriolanus |
| Volsci -orum (*m pl*) | Volscians |

Vocabulary

populus -i (*m*)	people
preces -ium (*f pl*)	prayers
oculus -i (*m*)	eye
decipio -ere	I deceive
captiva -ae (*f*)	(female) prisoner
permotus -a -um	moved, affected

Passage 9

Manlius Torquatus puts his duty as a general above his feelings as a father.

dum Romani contra <u>Latinos</u> pugnant, <u>Manlius Torquatus</u> exercitum ducebat; filius eius,
<u>Titus</u> nomine, <u>equitibus</u> <u>praeerat</u>. <u>Torquatus</u>, vir severus sed <u>pugna</u> fortissimus, suis
imperavit ne extra <u>ordinem</u> irent ut cum hostibus pugnarent. <u>disciplinam</u> enim militum
hoc modo <u>augere</u> volebat. <u>Titus</u> tamen prope <u>stationem</u> quandam <u>Latinorum</u> aderat. ibi
5　<u>Geminus Minucius</u>, <u>equitum</u> hostium dux, ridens dixit eum secum pugnare timere.
<u>Titus</u> igitur tam iratus erat ut, verborum patris oblitus, illum saevissime oppugnatum
necavit et arma cepit.

ubi in castra rediit, arma <u>Minucii</u> patri statim dedit. <u>Torquatus</u> tamen vultum a filio
avertit et '<u>Tite Manli</u>' inquit 'quod neque imperatori neque patri paruisti, te interfici
10　iubeo'. his verbis dictis omnes milites miseri erant. <u>Torquatum</u> enim ferocius egisse
credebant quam deberet. sed ex illo tempore ei semper parebant et officia sua
diligentius faciebant. <u>Latinis</u> igitur hoc anno superatis, <u>Torquatus</u> a militibus laudatus
est.

Names

Latini -orum (*m pl*)	Latins, people of Latium
Manlius -i Torquatus -i (*m*)	Manlius Torquatus (*also called just Torquatus*)
Titus -i (*m*)	Titus (*also called Titus Manlius*)
Geminus -i Minucius -i (*m*)	Geminus Minucius

Vocabulary

equites -um (*m pl*)	cavalry
praesum -esse	I am in charge of (+ *dat*)
pugna -ae (*f*)	fight, fighting
ordo -inis (*m*)	line
disciplina -ae (*f*)	discipline
augeo -ere	I increase (something)
statio -onis (*f*)	outpost

Passage 10

Papirius finds a way of dealing with his mother's curiosity.

mos antea erat senatoribus Romanis in curiam cum filiis intrare. ubi olim res magna
de qua senatores consulebant in posterum diem prolata est, mater Papirii pueri qui cum
patre in curia fuerat filium rogavit quid senatores agerent. omnes tamen qui in curia
aderant de hac re tacere iussi erant. itaque puer respondit se nihil dicturum esse. mater
5   tamen iterum atque iterum rogavit.

tandem igitur Papirius lepidam fabulam excogitavit. dixit enim senatores consulere
utrum unus vir duas uxores habere deberet, an una femina duos maritos. quod cum
mater audivisset, domo statim egressa aliis feminis nuntiavit quid filius dixisset. illae
igitur omnes ad curiam festinaverunt. cum advenissent orabant senatores ut una femina
10 duos maritos haberet. quae verba audita senatores mirati sunt quod nesciebant cur
feminae ita postularent. tum puer Papirius surrexit et omnibus narravit quid mater
rogavisset, quid ipse matri dixisset.

Names

      Papirius -i (*m*)   Papirius

Vocabulary

curia -ae (*f*)	senate-house
consulo -ere	I have a discussion
posterus -a -um	next, following
profero -ferre -tuli -latus	I postpone, I defer
lepidus -a -um	charming, witty
fabula -ae (*f*)	story
excogito -are -avi	I think up, I invent

Passage 11

Hannibal has a dream about his planned invasion of Italy.

Hannibal in Hispania contra socios Romanorum bellum gerebat. Romani enim ipsi hostes eius diu fuerant. cum urbem Saguntum cepisset, exercitum in Italiam ducere constituit ut Romam oppugnaret. ea nocte in somnio videbatur in concilium deorum vocari. ibi Hannibali, roganti quid sibi faciendum esset, Iuppiter imperavit ut quam
5 celerrime proficisceretur. rex deorum promisit se ei daturum esse ducem qui exercitum eius in Italiam duceret. hic dux Hannibali in eodem somnio apparuit et 'noli' inquit 'in itinere oculos revertere'.

ille tamen, haud longe progressus, cum suos in campo instructos videre cuperet, duci non paruit. tum a tergo conspexit monstrum ingens, quod omnes arbores et plurima
10 aedificia delebat. cum Hannibal miratus quaesivisset quid significaret tantum monstrum, dux respondet vastitatem Italiae esse. eum hortatus est ne curaret quid a tergo fieret sed Italiam sine mora peteret.

Names

Hannibal -alis (*m*)	Hannibal
Hispania -ae (*f*)	Spain
Saguntum -i (*n*)	Saguntum (*a city in Spain*)
Italia -ae (*f*)	Italy
Iuppiter (*m*)	Jupiter

Vocabulary

socius -i (*m*)	ally
somnium -i (*n*)	dream
concilium -i (*n*)	assembly, meeting
oculus -i (*m*)	eye
campus -i (*m*)	plain
tergum -i (*n*)	back
monstrum -i (*n*)	monster
aedificium -i (*n*)	building
significo -are	I mean, I signify
vastitas -atis (*f*)	devastation, destruction
mora -ae (*f*)	delay

Passage 12

Regulus puts the interests of Rome before his own.

tum Regulus dux, quem Carthaginienses ceperant, Romam missus est ut pacem ab eis
peteret et permutationem captivorum faceret. cum ad urbem advenisset, amici
gaudentes eum in curiam duxerunt. sed Regulus nihil quasi Romanus egit. dixit enim se,
ex illo die ubi in potestatem hostium venisset, civem Romanum esse desivisse. itaque
5 senatoribus persuasit ne pax cum Carthaginiensibus fieret. dixit enim hostes multis
cladibus fractos spem nullam habere. noluit plurimos eorum captivos reddi pro se et
paucis Romanis captis.

amici Regulo persuadere conati sunt ne Carthaginem rediret. uxorem igitur eius et filios
ad curiam invitaverunt. illa liberos marito ostendens oravit ut domi maneret. Regulus
10 tamen dixit se malle hostibus tradi. deinde Carthaginem rediit, quamquam sciebat
hostes se necaturos esse. Romani hostes pacem petentes accipere noluerunt. sic Regulus
summum fidei virtutisque exemplum omnibus qui aderant praebuit.

Names

Regulus -i (*m*)	Regulus
Carthaginienses -ium (*m pl*)	Carthaginians
Carthago -inis (*f*)	Carthage (*a city in North Africa*)

Vocabulary

permutatio -onis (*f*)	exchange
curia -ae (*f*)	senate-house
desino -ere desivi	I cease
clades -is (*f*)	disaster

Passage 13

A murder is revealed by dreams.

duo iuvenes iter per Graeciam olim faciebant. cum Megaram venissent, alter in taberna
alter apud amicum pernoctavit. dum hic dormit, ille apparere visus est et orare ut
adiuvaret, cum mors sibi a caupone pararetur. is somnio perterritus statim surrexit. mox
tamen, ubi intellexit se sine causa timere, iterum dormivit.

5   tum ei dormienti umbra amici iterum apparuit. 'occisus sum' inquit 'quod tu nihil fecisti.
sed quamquam me vivum non adiuvisti, mortuum vindica. caupo ille scelestus
puniendus est. nolo eum effugere posse.' dixit se interfectum in plaustrum iactum esse
fimo supra iniecto. petivit ut amicus prima luce ad portam oppidi adesset, priusquam
plaustrum exiret. quibus verbis commotus amicus surrexit et ad portam oppidi
10   festinavit. servum conspectum rogavit quid in plaustro esset. ille perterritus fugit, sed
corpore invento caupo poenas dedit.

Names

Graecia -ae (*f*)	Greece
Megara -ae (*f*)	Megara (*a town in Greece*)

Vocabulary

pernocto -are -avi	I spend the night
caupo -onis (*m*)	innkeeper
somnium -i (*n*)	dream
vindico -are	I avenge, I obtain vengeance for
plaustrum -i (*n*)	wagon, cart
fimus -i (*m*)	manure
supra	on top
commotus -a -um	disturbed

Passage 14

A band of robbers recruit a new leader, with unexpected results.

olim latrones oppidum oppugnaverunt et puellam pulchram ceperunt. quam cum
duxissent ad speluncam in qua habitabant, ibi captivam tenebant. puella tristissima erat,
quod amicum habebat, qui se in matrimonium ducere cupiebat. postquam dux latronum
in impetu necatus est, ceteri novum ducem quaerere constituerunt. paucis post diebus
5 iuvenem quendam, Haemum nomine, invenerunt. quod fortissimus esse videbatur, eum
primum oraverunt ut latro fieret, deinde principem fecerunt.

interea de puella consuluerunt: alii eam ancillam esse volebant, alii interficere ne
molesta esset. Haemus autem eis persuasit ut puellam in urbem ductam magno pretio
vendere conarentur. puella, simulac se non iam morituram esse cognovit, laetissima
10 fuit. illa nocte Haemus cena parata tantum vini latronibus dedit ut brevi tempore omnes
dormirent. ipse tamen neque vinum bibit neque dormivit, sed latronibus vinctis puellam
domum reduxit. latrones enim nesciebant Haemum sponsum puellae esse.

Name

Haemus -i (*m*)   Haemus

Vocabulary

latro -onis (*m*)   robber
spelunca -ae (*f*)   cave
captiva -ae (*f*)   (female) prisoner
in matrimonium duco   I marry
consulo -ere -ui   I consult, I have a discussion
molestus -a -um   troublesome
pretium -i (*n*)   price
vincio -ire vinxi vinctus   I tie (someone) up
sponsus -i (*m*)   fiance

Passage 15

Mycerinus finds a way to cheat the gods.

Mycerinus, ut dicitur, rex Aegyptiorum factus, nuntios ad oraculum Iovis misit, cum a deo cognoscere vellet quot annos victurus esset. deus respondit Mycerinum, cum sex annos rexisset, subito periturum esse. quae verba miratus ille 'dei me decipiunt' inquit 'nam pater et avunculus meus, qui populum multis iniuriis opprimebant, diu vixerunt;
5   mihi tamen bene et fideliter regenti Iuppiter vitam brevissimam dedit'.

tum nuntiis imperavit ut ad oraculum iterum irent et a deo peterent cur pietas sua ita puniretur. illi regressi nuntiaverunt deum iratum esse, cum ipse constituisset Aegyptios centum annos crudelia passuros esse. itaque Mycerinus, cum se diu victurum esse non iam speraret, multas lucernas paravit ut per noctes, sicut per dies, conviviis sine fine
10   frueretur. 'hoc modo' inquit 'ego deos decipiam et sex annos ab eis mihi datos sic duplicabo'.

Names

Mycerinus -i (*m*)	Mycerinus
Aegyptii -orum (*m pl*)	Egyptians
Iupiter Iovis (*m*)	Jupiter

Vocabulary

decipio -ere	I cheat (someone)
avunculus -i (*m*)	uncle
pietas -atis (*f*)	dutiful behaviour
lucerna -ae (*f*)	lamp
sicut	just as, just like
convivium -i (*n*)	feast
fruor -i	I enjoy (+ *abl*)
decipio -ere	I cheat (someone)
duplico -are	I double

Vocabulary

The second column has further information about each word:

• Verbs are shown with principal parts (see page 53): present tense (first person singular) in the first column, then infinitive (showing conjugation, e.g. 3rd), perfect tense (first person singular), and perfect passive participle. Note that 3rd* = mixed 3rd/4th conjugation: these verbs count as 3rd because of infinitive *-ere*, but form present, imperfect and future tenses like 4th (see page 46).

• Nouns are shown with genitive singular, gender, and declension (e.g. 3).

• Adjectives are given with feminine and neuter. If only one other form is given, it is the neuter (and the feminine is the same as the masculine). A few third declension adjectives are shown instead with the genitive singular (for the stem).

• Common irregular forms are cross-referenced.

• For explanation of abbreviations, see the list on page viii.

a/ab	+ *abl, or as prefix*	*prep*	from, by
abstuli		(*perfect of* aufero)	
absum	abesse, afui	*verb irreg*	be out, be absent, be away
ac/atque	*indecl*	*conj*	and
accepi		(*perfect of* accipio)	
accido	accidere, accidi	*verb 3rd*	happen
accipio	accipere, accepi, acceptus	*verb 3rd**	accept, take in, receive
acriter	*indecl*	*adv*	keenly, eagerly, fiercely
actus	acta, actum	(*perfect passive participle of* ago)	
ad	+ *acc, or as prefix*	*prep*	to, towards, at
adeo	*indecl*	*adv*	so much, so greatly
adiuvo	adiuvare, adiuvi, adiutus	*verb 1st*	help
adsum	adesse, adfui	*verb irreg*	be here, be present
advenio	advenire, adveni	*verb 4th*	arrive
aedifico	aedificare, aedificavi, -atus	*verb 1st*	build
aequus	aequa, aequum	*adj*	equal, fair, calm
ager	agri	*noun m 2*	field
ago	agere, egi, actus	*verb 3rd*	do, act
aliquis	aliquid	*pron*	someone, something
alius	alia, aliud	*adj/pron*	other, another, else
alii ... alii			some ... others (*see page 39*)
alter	altera, alterum	*adj/pron*	the other, another, second of two
alter ... alter			one ... the other (*of two*)
altus	alta, altum	*adj*	high, deep
ambulo	ambulare, ambulavi	*verb 1st*	walk
amicus	amici	*noun m 2*	friend
amo	amare, amavi, amatus	*verb 1st*	love, like
amor	amoris	*noun m 3*	love
ancilla	ancillae	*noun f 1*	slave-girl, maid
animadverto	animadvertere, -verti, -versus	*verb 3rd*	notice, take notice of
animus	animi	*noun m 2*	mind, spirit, soul

annus	anni	*noun m 2*	year
ante	*+ acc*	*prep*	before, in front of
antea	*indecl*	*adv*	before, previously
aperio	aperire, aperui, apertus	*verb 4th*	open
appareo	apparere, apparui	*verb 2nd*	appear
appropinquo	appropinquare, -quavi, -quatus	*verb 1st*	approach, come near to
apud	*+ acc*	*prep*	among, with, at the house of
aqua	aquae	*noun f 1*	water
arbor	arboris	*noun f 3*	tree
argentum	argenti	*noun n 2*	silver
arma	armorum	*noun n 2 pl*	arms, weapons
ars	artis	*noun f 3*	art, skill
ascendo	ascendere, ascendi, ascensus	*verb 3rd*	climb
audax	*gen* audacis	*adj*	bold, daring
audeo	audere, ausus sum	*verb 2nd s-dep*	dare
audio	audire, audivi, auditus	*verb 4th*	hear, listen to
aufero	auferre, abstuli, ablatus	*verb irreg*	take away, carry off, steal
augeo	augere, auxi, auctus	*verb 2nd*	increase
aurum	auri	*noun n 2*	gold
aut ... aut	*indecl*	*conj*	either ... or
autem	*indecl*	*conj*	however, but
auxilium	auxilii	*noun n 2*	help
bellum	belli	*noun n 2*	war
bellum gero			wage war, campaign
bene	*indecl*	*adv*	well
benignus	benigna, benignum	*adj*	kind
bibo	bibere, bibi	*verb 3rd*	drink
bonus	bona, bonum	*adj*	good
bona	bonorum	*noun n 2 pl*	goods
melior	melius	*adj*	better
optimus	optima, optimum	*adj*	best, excellent, very good
brevis	breve	*adj*	short, brief
cado	cadere, cecidi	*verb 3rd*	fall
caelum	caeli	*noun n 2*	sky, heaven
capio	capere, cepi, captus	*verb 3rd**	take, catch, capture
captivus	captivi	*noun m 2*	captive, prisoner
captus	capta, captum	*(perfect passive participle of* capio)	
caput	capitis	*noun n 3*	head
carus	cara, carum	*adj*	dear
castra	castrorum	*noun n 2 pl*	camp
causa	causae	*noun 1 f*	cause, reason; case (in court)
cecidi		*(perfect of* cado)	
celer	celeris, celere	*adj*	quick, fast
celo	celare, celavi, celatus	*verb 1st*	hide
cena	cenae	*noun f 1*	dinner

centum	*indecl*	*num*	100
cepi		*(perfect of* capio)	
ceteri	ceterae, cetera	*adj/pron*	the rest, the others
cibus	cibi	*noun m 2*	food
circum	*+ acc*	*prep*	around
civis	civis	*noun m/f 3*	citizen
clamo	clamare, clamavi, clamatus	*verb 1st*	shout
clamor	clamoris	*noun m 3*	shout, shouting, noise
clarus	clara, clarum	*adj*	famous, distinguished
coactus	coacta, coactum	*(perfect passive participle of* cogo)	
coegi		*(perfect of* cogo)	
coepi	coepisse, coeptus	*verb irreg*	began *(perfect: see page 63)*
cogito	cogitare, cogitavi, cogitatus	*verb 1st*	think, consider
cognosco	cognoscere, cognovi, cognitus	*verb 3rd*	get to know, find out
cogo	cogere, coegi, coactus	*verb 3rd*	force, compel
comes	comitis	*noun m/f 3*	comrade, companion
conficio	conficere, confeci, confectus	*verb 3rd**	finish; wear out, exhaust
conor	conari, conatus sum	*verb 1st dep*	try
consilium	consilii	*noun n 2*	plan, idea, advice
conspectus	conspecta, conspectum	*(perfect passive participle of* conspicio)	
conspexi		*(perfect of* conspicio)	
conspicio	conspicere, conspexi, -spectus	*verb 3rd**	catch sight of, notice
constituo	constituere, constitui, -utus	*verb 3rd*	decide
consumo	consumere, consumpsi, -sumptus	*verb 3rd*	eat
contra	*+ acc*	*prep*	against
convenio	convenire, conveni, conventus	*verb 4th*	come together, gather, meet
copiae	copiarum	*noun f 1 pl*	forces, troops
corpus	corporis	*noun n 3*	body
credo	credere, credidi, creditus	*verb 3rd*	believe, trust, have faith in *(+ dat)*
crudelis	crudele	*adj*	cruel
cucurri		*(perfect of* curro)	
culpo	culpare, culpavi, culpatus	*verb 1st*	blame
cum	*indecl*	*conj*	when
cum	*+ abl*	*prep*	with
cupio	cupere, cupivi	*verb 3rd**	want, desire
cur?	*indecl*	*adv*	why?
cura	curae	*noun 1 f*	care, worry
curo	curare, curavi, curatus	*verb 1st*	look after, care for, supervise
curro	currere, cucurri, cursus	*verb 3rd*	run
custodio	custodire, custodivi, custoditus	*verb 4th*	guard
custos	custodis	*noun m/f 3*	guard
datus	data, datum	*(perfect passive participle of* do)	
de	*+ abl*	*prep*	from, down from; about
dea	deae	*noun f 1*	goddess
debeo	debere, debui, debitus	*verb 2nd*	owe, ought, should, must
decem	*indecl*	*num*	ten

dedi		*(perfect of* do)	
defendo	defendere, defendi, defensus	*verb 3rd*	defend
deicio	deicere, deieci, deiectus	*verb 3rd**	throw down
deinde	*indecl*	*adv*	then, next
deleo	delere, delevi, deletus	*verb 2nd*	destroy
descendo	descendere, descendi, descensus	*verb 3rd*	go down, come down
deus	dei	*noun m 2*	god
dico	dicere, dixi, dictus	*verb 3rd*	say
dies	diei	*noun m/f 5*	day
difficilis	difficile	*adj*	difficult
dignitas	dignitatis	*noun f 3*	dignity, importance, honour, prestige
diligenter	*indecl*	*adv*	carefully
dirus	dira, dirum	*adj*	dreadful
discedo	discedere, discessi	*verb 3rd*	depart, leave
diu	*indecl*	*adv*	for a long time
dixi		*(perfect of* dico)	
do	dare, dedi, datus	*verb 1st*	give
poenas do			pay the penalty, be punished
doceo	docere, docui, doctus	*verb 2nd*	teach
dolor	doloris	*noun m 3*	pain, grief
domina	dominae	*noun f 1*	mistress
dominus	domini	*noun m 2*	master
domus	domus (domi = at home)	*noun f 4*	house, home
donum	doni	*noun n 2*	gift, present
dormio	dormire, dormivi	*verb 4th*	sleep
dubito	dubitare, dubitavi, dubitatus	*verb 1st*	hesitate, doubt
duco	ducere, duxi, ductus	*verb 3rd*	lead, take
dum	*indecl*	*conj*	while, until
duo	duae, duo	*num*	two
durus	dura, durum	*adj*	hard
dux	ducis	*noun m 3*	leader
duxi		*(perfect of* duco)	
e/ex	+ *abl, or as prefix*	*prep*	from, out of
ecce!	*indecl*	*interjection*	see! look!
effugio	effugere, effugi	*verb 3rd**	escape
egi		*(perfect of* ago)	
ego	mei	*pron*	I, me
egredior	egredi, egressus sum	*verb 3rd* dep*	go out
eicio	eicere, eieci, eiectus	*verb 3rd*	throw out
emo	emere, emi, emptus	*verb 3rd*	buy
enim	*indecl*	*conj*	for
eo	ire, i(v)i	*verb irreg*	go
epistula	epistulae	*noun f 1*	letter
equus	equi	*noun m 2*	horse
erumpo	erumpere, erupi, eruptus	*verb 3rd*	burst out

et	*indecl*	*conj*	and
et ... et			both ... and
etiam	*indecl*	*adv*	also, even
eunt-		(*stem of present participle of* eo)	
exemplum	exempli	*noun n 2*	example
exercitus	exercitus	*noun m 4*	army
expello	expellere, expuli, expulsus	*verb 3rd*	drive out
exspecto	exspectare, exspectavi, -atus	*verb 1st*	wait for
extra	+ *acc*	*prep*	outside
facilis	facile	*adj*	easy
facio	facere, feci, factus	*verb 3rd**	make, do
faveo	favere, favi	*verb 2nd*	favour, support (+ *dat*)
feci		(*perfect of* facio)	
felix	*gen* felicis	*adj*	fortunate, happy
femina	feminae	*noun f 1*	woman
fero	ferre, tuli, latus	*verb irreg*	bring, carry
ferox	*gen* ferocis	*adj*	fierce, ferocious
ferrum	ferri	*noun n 2*	iron, sword
festino	festinare, festinavi	*verb 1st*	hurry
fidelis	fidele	*adj*	faithful, loyal
fides	fidei	*noun f 5*	loyalty, trustworthiness
filia	filiae	*noun f 1*	daughter
filius	filii	*noun m 2*	son
finis	finis	*noun m 3*	end, boundary
fio	fieri, factus sum	*verb irreg s-dep*	become, be made
flumen	fluminis	*noun n 3*	river
forte	*indecl*	*adv*	by chance
fortis	forte	*adj*	brave
forum	fori	*noun n 2*	forum, marketplace
frango	frangere, fregi, fractus	*verb 3rd*	break
frater	fratris	*noun m 3*	brother
fregi		(*perfect of* frango)	
frustra	*indecl*	*adv*	in vain
fudi		(*perfect of* fundo)	
fugio	fugere, fugi	*verb 3rd**	run away, flee
fui		(*perfect of* sum)	
fundo	fundere, fudi, fusus	*verb 3rd*	pour
gaudeo	gaudere, gavisus sum	*verb 2nd s-dep*	rejoice, be pleased
gaudium	gaudii	*noun n 2*	joy, pleasure
gens	gentis	*noun f 3*	family, tribe, race, people
gero	gerere, gessi, gestus	*verb 3rd*	wage (war); wear (clothes)
bellum gero			wage war, campaign
gladius	gladii	*noun m 2*	sword
gravis	grave	*adj*	heavy, serious

habeo	habere, habui, habitus	*verb 2nd*	have
habito	habitare, habitavi, habitatus	*verb 1st*	live (in), inhabit
hasta	hastae	*noun f 1*	spear
haud	*indecl*	*adv*	not
heri	*indecl*	*adv*	yesterday
hic	haec, hoc	*pron/adj*	this
hic	*indecl*	*adv*	here
hodie	*indecl*	*adv*	today
homo	hominis	*noun m 3*	man, human being
hora	horae	*noun f 1*	hour
hortor	hortari, hortatus sum	*verb 1st dep*	encourage, urge
hortus	horti	*noun m 2*	garden
hostis	hostis	*noun m 3*	enemy
humus	humi (humi = on the ground)	*noun f 2*	ground
iaceo	iacere, iacui	*verb 2nd*	lie
iacio	iacere, ieci, iactus	*verb 3rd**	throw
deicio	deicere, deieci, deiectus	*verb 3rd**	throw down
eicio	eicere, eieci, eiectus	*verb 3rd*	throw out
inicio	inicere, inieci, iniectus	*verb 3rd*	throw in
iactus	iacta, iactum	*(perfect passive participle of* iacio*)*	
iam	*indecl*	*adv*	now, already
ianua	ianuae	*noun f 1*	door
ibi	*indecl*	*adv*	there
idem	eadem, idem	*pron/adj*	the same
ieci		*(perfect of* iacio*)*	
iens	*gen* euntis	*(present participle of* eo*)*	
igitur	*indecl*	*conj*	therefore
ignis	ignis	*noun m 3*	fire
ii		*(=* ivi, *perfect of* eo*)*	
ille	illa, illud	*pron/adj*	that; he, she, it
impedio	impedire, impedivi, impeditus	*verb 4th*	hinder
imperator	imperatoris	*noun m 3*	commander; emperor
imperium	imperii	*noun n 2*	empire, power, command
impero	imperare, imperavi, imperatus	*verb 1st*	order, command (+ *dat*)
impetus	impetus	*noun m 4*	attack
in	+ *acc/abl*	*prep*	(+ *acc*) into; (+ *abl*) in
incendo	incendere, incendi, incensus	*verb 3rd*	burn, set on fire
incipio	incipere, incepi, inceptus	*verb 3rd**	begin
infelix	*gen* infelicis	*adj*	unlucky, unhappy
ingenium	ingenii	*noun n 2*	character
ingens	*gen* ingentis	*adj*	huge
ingredior	ingredi, ingressus sum	*verb 3rd* dep*	enter
inicio	inicere, inieci, iniectus	*verb 3rd*	throw in
inimicus	inimici	*noun m 2*	enemy (*usu* personal)
iniuria	iniuriae	*noun f 1*	injustice, injury
inquit	*pl* inquiunt	*verb irreg*	(he) says, (he) said

instruo	instruere, instruxi, instructus	*verb 3rd*	draw up, arrange, set up
insula	insulae	*noun f 1*	island; block of flats
intellego	intellegere, intellexi, intellectus	*verb 3rd*	understand
inter	+ *acc*	*prep*	among
interea	*indecl*	*adv*	meanwhile
interficio	interficere, interfeci, interfectus	*verb 3rd**	kill
intra	+ *acc*	*prep*	inside
intro	intrare, intravi, intratus	*verb 1st*	enter
invenio	invenire, inveni, inventus	*verb 4th*	find
invito	invitare, invitavi, invitatus	*verb 1st*	invite
ipse	ipsa, ipsum	*pron*	self (*any person*), himself, herself, itself, *pl* selves, themselves
ira	irae	*noun f 1*	anger
iratus	irata, iratum	*adj*	angry
irrumpo	irrumpere, irrupi, irruptus	*verb 3rd*	burst in
is	ea, id	*pron*	he, she, it, *pl* they; that, *pl* those
ita	*indecl*	*adv*	in this way
itaque	*indecl*	*conj*	and so, therefore
iter	itineris	*noun n 3*	journey
iterum	*indecl*	*adv*	again
iubeo	iubere, iussi, iussus	*verb 2nd*	order
iussi		(*perfect of* iubeo)	
iussus	iussa, iussum	(*perfect passive participle of* iubeo)	
iuvenis	iuvenis	*noun m 3*	young man
ivi		(*perfect of* eo)	
labor	laboris	*noun m 3*	work
laboro	laborare, laboravi	*verb 1st*	work
lacrima	lacrimae	*noun f 1*	tear
lacrimo	lacrimare, lacrimavi	*verb 1st*	weep, cry
laetus	laeta, laetum	*adj*	happy
latus (i)	lata, latum	*adj*	wide
latus (ii)	lata, latum	(*perfect passive participle of* fero)	
laudo	laudare, laudavi, laudatus	*verb 1st*	praise
lectus	lecta, lectum	(*perfect passive participle of* lego)	
legatus	legati	*noun m 2*	commander
legio	legionis	*noun f 3*	legion
lego	legere, legi, lectus	*verb 3rd*	read; choose
lente	*indecl*	*adv*	slowly
levis	leve	*adj*	light, slight, trivial
lex	legis	*noun f 3*	law
libenter	*indecl*	*adv*	willingly, gladly
liber	libri	*noun m 2*	book
liberi	liberorum	*noun m 2 pl*	children
libero	liberare, liberavi, liberatus	*verb 1st*	free, set free
libertas	libertatis	*noun f 3*	freedom
libertus	liberti	*noun m 2*	freedman, ex-slave

locus	loci (*pl is n:* loca)	*noun m/n 2*	place
locutus sum		*(perfect of* loquor*)*	
longus	longa, longum	*adj*	long
loquor	loqui, locutus sum	*verb 3rd dep*	speak
lux	lucis	*noun f 3*	light, daylight
magis	*indecl*	*adv*	more
magister	magistri	*noun m 2*	master, schoolmaster, foreman
magnus	magna, magnum	*adj*	big, large, great
maior	maius	*adj*	bigger, greater
maximus	maxima, maximum	*adj*	biggest, greatest, very big/great
malo	malle, malui	*verb irreg*	prefer
malus	mala, malum	*adj*	bad, evil
peior	peius	*adj*	worse
pessimus	pessima, pessimum	*adj*	worst, very bad
maneo	manere, mansi	*verb 2nd*	remain, stay
mansi		*(perfect of* maneo*)*	
manus	manus	*noun f 4*	hand; group of people
mare	maris	*noun n 3*	sea
maritus	mariti	*noun m 2*	husband
mater	matris	*noun f 3*	mother
maximus	maxima, maximum	*adj*	biggest, greatest, very big/great
medius	media, medium	*adj*	middle (of)
melior	melius	*adj*	better
mens	mentis	*noun f 3*	mind
metus	metus	*noun m 4*	fear
meus	mea, meum	*adj*	my
miles	militis	*noun m 3*	soldier
mille	*pl* milia	*num*	1000
minime	*indecl*	*adv*	no; least, very little
minimus	minima, minimum	*adj*	very little, smallest
minor	minus	*adj*	smaller, less
miror	mirari, miratus sum	*verb 1st dep*	wonder at, admire
miser	misera, miserum	*adj*	miserable, wretched, sad
misi		*(perfect of* mitto*)*	
missus	missa, missum	*(perfect passive participle of* mitto*)*	
mitto	mittere, misi, missus	*verb 3rd*	send
modus	modi	*noun m 2*	manner, way, kind
moneo	monere, monui, monitus	*verb 2nd*	warn, advise
mons	montis	*noun m 3*	mountain
morbus	morbi	*noun m 2*	illness
morior	mori, mortuus sum	*verb 3rd* dep*	die
mors	mortis	*noun f 3*	death
mortuus sum		*(perfect of* morior*)*	
mos	moris	*noun m 3*	custom
motus	mota, motum	*(perfect passive participle of* moveo*)*	
moveo	movere, movi, motus	*verb 2nd*	move

mox	*indecl*	*adv*	soon
multitudo	multitudinis	*noun f 3*	crowd
multus	multa, multum	*adj*	much, *pl* many
multo	*indecl*	*adv*	much, by much
plus	*gen* pluris	*adj*	more (of) (+ *gen*); *pl* more
plurimus	plurima, plurimum	*adj*	very much, *pl* very many, most
murus	muri	*noun m 2*	wall
muto	mutare, mutavi, mutatus	*verb 1st*	change
nam	*indecl*	*conj*	for
narro	narrare, narravi, narratus	*verb 1st*	tell, relate
nauta	nautae	*noun m 1*	sailor
navigo	navigare, navigavi	*verb 1st*	sail
navis	navis	*noun f 3*	ship
-ne ... ?	*indecl*	*adv*	(*makes open question, e.g.*) is it?
ne	*indecl*	*conj*	(that/so that) not
nec ... nec/neque ... neque *indecl*		*conj*	neither ... nor
neco	necare, necavi, necatus	*verb 1st*	kill
nemo	neminis	*irreg pron m/f*	no-one
nescio	nescire, nescivi	*verb 4th*	not know
nihil	*indecl*	*irreg pron n*	nothing
nisi	*indecl*	*conj*	unless, except
noceo	nocere, nocui	*verb 2nd*	harm, hurt (+ *dat*)
nolo	nolle, nolui	*verb irreg*	not want
nomen	nominis	*noun n 3*	name
non	*indecl*	*adv*	not
nonne ... ?	*indecl*	*adv*	surely?
nonnulli	nonnullae, nonnulla	*adj*	some, several
nos	nostrum	*pron*	we, us
noster	nostra, nostrum	*adj*	our
novem	*indecl*	*num*	nine
novus	nova, novum	*adj*	new
nox	noctis	*noun f 3*	night
nullus	nulla, nullum	*adj*	no ... , not any
num	*indecl*	*adv*	whether (*in indirect question*)
num ... ?	*indecl*	*adv*	surely ... not?
numquam	*indecl*	*adv*	never
nunc	*indecl*	*adv*	now
nuntio	nuntiare, nuntiavi, nuntiatus	*verb 1st*	announce
nuntius	nuntii	*noun m 2*	messenger, message, news
oblatus	oblata, oblatum	(*perfect passive participle of* offero)	
obliviscor	oblivisci, oblitus sum	*verb 3rd dep*	forget (+ *gen*)
obtuli		(*perfect of* offero)	
occido	occidere, occidi, occisus	*verb 3rd*	kill
octo	*indecl*	*num*	eight
odi	odisse	*verb irreg (perf form)*	hate (*see page 63*)

offero	offere, obtuli, oblatus	*verb irreg*	offer
officium	officii	*noun n 2*	business, duty, service
olim	*indecl*	*adv*	once, some time ago
omnis	omne	*adj*	all, every
oppidum	oppidi	*noun n 2*	town
opprimo	opprimere, oppressi, oppressus	*verb 3rd*	crush
oppugno	oppugnare, oppugnavi, -atus	*verb 1st*	attack
optimus	optima, optimum	*adj*	best, excellent, very good
oratio	orationis	*noun f 3*	speech
orior	oriri, ortus sum	*verb 4th dep*	rise up, arise
oro	orare, oravi, oratus	*verb 1st*	beg
ostendo	ostendere, ostendi, ostentus	*verb 3rd*	show
paene	*indecl*	*adv*	almost, nearly
parco	parcere, peperci	*verb 3rd*	spare (+ *dat*)
pareo	parere, parui	*verb 2nd*	obey (+ *dat*)
paro	parare, paravi, paratus	*verb 1st*	prepare
pars	partis	*noun f 3*	part
parvus	parva, parvum	*adj*	small
minor	minus	*adj*	smaller, less
minimus	minima, minimum	*adj*	very little, smallest
minime	*indecl*	*adv*	no; least, very little
passus sum		(*perfect of* patior)	
pater	patris	*noun m 3*	father
patior	pati, passus sum	*verb 3rd dep*	suffer, endure
patria	patriae	*noun f 1*	homeland, fatherland, country
pauci	paucae, pauca	*adj pl*	few
paulisper	*indecl*	*adv*	for a short time
paulo/paulum	*indecl*	*adv*	a little
pax	pacis	*noun f 3*	peace
pecunia	pecuniae	*noun f 1*	money
peior	peius	*adj*	worse
pello	pellere, pepuli, pulsus	*verb 3rd*	drive
expello	expellere, expuli, expulsus	*verb 3rd*	drive out
repello	repellere, reppuli, repulsus	*verb 3rd*	drive back
peperci		(*perfect of* parco)	
per	+ *acc*	*prep*	through, along
pereo	perire, perii	*verb irreg*	die, perish
perfidia	perfidiae	*noun f 1*	treachery
perfidus	perfida, perfidum	*adj*	treacherous, untrustworthy
periculum	periculi	*noun n 2*	danger
permitto	permittere, permisi, permissus	*verb 3rd*	allow (+ *dat*)
persuadeo	persuadere, persuasi	*verb 2nd*	persuade (+ *dat*)
perterritus	perterrita, perterritum	*adj*	terrified
pervenio	pervenire, perveni	*verb 4th*	reach, arrive at
pes	pedis	*noun m 3*	foot
pessimus	pessima, pessimum	*adj*	worst, very bad

peto	petere, petivi, petitus	*verb 3rd*	seek, ask for, make for, attack
placet	placere, placuit	*verb 2nd impsl*	it pleases, it suits (+ *dat*)
plenus	plena, plenum	*adj*	full
plus	*gen* pluris	*adj*	more of (+ *gen*); *pl* more
plurimus	plurima, plurimum	*adj*	very much, *pl* very many, most
poena	poenae	*noun f 1*	punishment
poenas do			pay the penalty, be punished
pono	ponere, posui, positus	*verb 3rd*	place, put, put up
porta	portae	*noun f 1*	gate
porto	portare, portavi, portatus	*verb 1st*	carry
portus	portus	*noun m 4*	harbour, port
positus	posita, positum	(*perfect passive participle of* pono)	
possum	posse, potui	*verb irreg*	can, be able
post	+ *acc*	*prep*	after
postea	*indecl*	*adv*	afterwards
postquam	*indecl*	*conj*	after, when
postridie	*indecl*	*adv*	on the next day
postulo	postulare, postulavi, postulatus	*verb 1st*	demand
posui		(*perfect of* pono)	
potens	*gen* potentis	*adj*	powerful
potestas	potestatis	*noun f 3*	power
potui		(*perfect of* possum)	
praebeo	praebere, praebui, praebitus	*verb 2nd*	provide
praemium	praemii	*noun n 2*	prize, reward, profit
praeter	+ *acc*	*prep*	except
precor	precari, precatus sum	*verb 1st dep*	pray (to)
primo	*indecl*	*adv*	at first
primus	prima, primum	*adj*	first
princeps	principis	*noun m 3*	chief, chieftain, emperor
priusquam	*indecl*	*conj*	before, until
pro	+ *abl*	*prep*	in front of, for, in return for
procedo	procedere, processi	*verb 3rd*	advance, proceed
proelium	proelii	*noun n 2*	battle
proficiscor	proficisci, profectus sum	*verb 3rd dep*	set out
progredior	progredi, progressus sum	*verb 3rd dep*	advance
promitto	promittere, promisi, promissus	*verb 3rd*	promise
prope	+ *acc*	*prep*	near
propter	+ *acc*	*prep*	on account of, because of
proximus	proxima, proximum	*adj*	nearest, next to
puella	puellae	*noun f 1*	girl
puer	pueri	*noun m 2*	boy
pugno	pugnare, pugnavi	*verb 1st*	fight
pulcher	pulchra, pulchrum	*adj*	beautiful, handsome
punio	punire, punivi, punitus	*verb 4th*	punish
puto	putare, putavi, putatus	*verb 1st*	think
quaero	quaerere, quaesivi, quaesitus	*verb 3rd*	search for, look for, ask

qualis?	quale?	*adj*	what sort of?
quam (i)	*indecl*	*adv*	how ... ! how ... ?
quam celerrime			as quickly as possible
quam (ii)	*indecl*	*adv*	than
quamquam	*conj*		although
quantus?	quanta? quantum?	*adj*	how big?
quasi	*indecl*	*adv*	as if
quattuor	*indecl*	*num*	four
-que	*indecl*	*conj*	and (*before word it is attached to*)
qui	quae, quod	*pron*	who, which
quidam	quaedam, quoddam	*pron*	a certain, one, some
quies	quietis	*noun f 3*	rest
quinque	*indecl*	*num*	five
quis?	quid?	*pron*	who? what?
quo?	*indecl*	*adv*	where to?
quod	*indecl*	*conj*	because
quo modo?	*indecl*	*adv*	in what way? how?
quondam	*indecl*	*adv*	one day, once
quoque	*indecl*	*conj*	also, too
quot?	*indecl*	*adj*	how many?
rapio	rapere, rapui, raptus	*verb 3rd**	seize, grab
re-	*indecl*	*prefix*	... back
reddo	reddere, reddidi, redditus	*verb 3rd*	give back, restore
redeo	redire, redii	*verb irreg*	go back, come back, return
refero	referre, rettuli, relatus	*verb irreg*	bring/carry back; report, tell
regina	reginae	*noun f 1*	queen
regnum	regni	*noun n 2*	kingdom
rego	regere, rexi, rectus	*verb 3rd*	rule, reign
regredior	regredi, regressus sum	*verb 3rd* dep*	go back, return
relinquo	relinquere, reliqui, relictus	*verb 3rd*	leave, leave behind
repello	repellere, reppuli, repulsus	*verb 3rd*	drive back
res	rei	*noun f 5*	thing, business
resisto	resistere, restiti	*verb 3rd*	resist (+ *dat*)
respondeo	respondere, respondi, responsus	*verb 2nd*	reply
rex	regis	*noun 3 m*	king
rideo	ridere, risi	*verb 2nd*	laugh, smile
risi		(*perfect of* rideo)	
rogo	rogare, rogavi, rogatus	*verb 1st*	ask, ask for
Roma	Romae (Romae = at/in Rome)	*noun f 1*	Rome
Romanus	Romana, Romanum	*adj*	Roman
rumpo	rumpere, rupi, ruptus	*verb 3rd*	burst
erumpo	erumpere, erupi, eruptus	*verb 3rd*	burst out
irrumpo	irrumpere, irrupi, irruptus	*verb 3rd*	burst in
sacer	sacra, sacrum	*adj*	sacred
saepe	*indecl*	*adv*	often

saevus	saeva, saevum	*adj*	savage, cruel
saluto	salutare, salutavi, salutatus	*verb 1st*	greet
salve!	*pl* salvete!	*imperat*	hello!
sanguis	sanguinis	*noun m 3*	blood
sapiens	*gen* sapientis	*adj*	wise
satis	*indecl*	*adv*	enough
scelestus	scelesta, scelestum	*adj*	wicked
scelus	sceleris	*noun n 3*	crime
scio	scire, scivi, scitus	*verb 4th*	know
scribo	scribere, scripsi, scriptus	*verb 3rd*	write
scripsi		*(perfect of* scribo)	
se	sui	*refl pron*	himself, herself, itself, themselves
secutus sum		*(perfect of* sequor)	
sed	*indecl*	*conj*	but
sedeo	sedere, sedi	*verb 2nd*	sit
semper	*indecl*	*adv*	always
senator	senatoris	*noun m 3*	senator
senatus	senatus	*noun m 4*	the senate
senex	senis	*noun m 3*	old man
sentio	sentire, sensi, sensus	*verb 4th*	feel, notice
septem	*indecl*	*num*	seven
sequor	sequi, secutus sum	*verb 3rd dep*	follow
servo	servare, servavi, servatus	*verb 1st*	save, look after
servus	servi	*noun m 2*	slave
severus	severa, severum	*adj*	severe, strict
sex	*indecl*	*num*	six
si	*indecl*	*conj*	if
sic	*indecl*	*adv*	thus, in this way
signum	signi	*noun n 2*	sign, signal, seal
silentium	silentii	*noun n 2*	silence
silva	silvae	*noun f 1*	wood
similis	simile	*adj*	similar (to), like (+ *dat*)
simul	*indecl*	*adv*	at the same time
simulac/simulatque	*indecl*	*conj*	as soon as
sine	+ *abl*	*prep*	without
soleo	solere, solitus sum	*verb 2nd s-dep*	be accustomed
solus	sola, solum	*adj*	alone, on one's own, lonely, only
specto	spectare, spectavi, spectatus	*verb 1st*	look at, watch
spero	sperare, speravi, speratus	*verb 1st*	hope, expect
spes	spei	*noun f 5*	hope
statim	*indecl*	*adv*	at once, immediately
steti		*(perfect of* sto)	
sto	stare, steti	*verb 1st*	stand
strepitus	strepitus	*noun m 4*	noise, din
stultus	stulta, stultum	*adj*	stupid, foolish
sub	+ *acc/abl*	*prep*	under, beneath
subito	*indecl*	*adv*	suddenly

Vocabulary

sum	esse, fui	*verb irreg*	be
summus	summa, summum	*adj*	highest, greatest, top (of)
supero	superare, superavi, superatus	*verb 1st*	overcome, overpower
surgo	surgere, surrexi	*verb 3rd*	get up, stand up, rise
surrexi		(*perfect of* surgo)	
suscipio	suscipere, suscepi, susceptus	*verb 3rd**	undertake, take on
sustuli		(*perfect of* tollo)	
suus	sua, suum	*adj*	his, her, its, their (own) (*refl*)
taberna	tabernae	*noun f 1*	shop, inn
taceo	tacere, tacui	*verb 2nd*	be silent, keep quiet
talis	tale	*adj*	such, of such a sort
tam	*indecl*	*adv*	so
tamen	*indecl*	*adv*	however
tandem	*indecl*	*adv*	at last, finally
tango	tangere, tetigi, tactus	*verb 3rd*	touch
tantus	tanta, tantum	*adj*	so great, such a great
tempestas	tempestas	*noun f 3*	storm
templum	templi	*noun n 2*	temple
tempus	temporis	*noun n 3*	time
teneo	tenere, tenui, tentus	*verb 2nd*	hold
terra	terrae	*noun f 1*	earth, land, ground
terreo	terrere, terrui, territus	*verb 2nd*	frighten
timeo	timere, timui	*verb 2nd*	fear, be afraid
tollo	tollere, sustuli, sublatus	*verb 3rd*	raise, lift up, hold up
tot	*indecl*	*adj*	so many
totus	tota, totum	*adj*	whole
trado	tradere, tradidi, traditus	*verb 3rd*	hand over
traho	trahere, traxi, tractus	*verb 3rd*	drag
trans	+ *acc, or as prefix*	*prep*	across
traxi		(*perfect of* traho)	
tres	tria	*num*	three
tristis	triste	*adj*	sad
tu	tui	*pron*	you (*sg*)
tuli		(*perfect of* fero)	
tum	*indecl*	*adv*	then, at that time
turba	turbae	*noun f 1*	crowd
tuus	tua, tuum	*adj*	your (of you *sg*), yours
ubi	*indecl*	*adv*	where, when; where?
ullus	ulla, ullum	*adj*	any
umbra	umbrae	*noun f 1*	shadow, ghost
umquam	*indecl*	*adv*	ever
unde	*indecl*	*adv*	from where
unus	una, unum	*num*	one
urbs	urbis	*noun f 3*	city
usus sum		(*perfect of* utor)	

Vocabulary

ut	*indecl*	*conj*	(+ *subjunctive*) that, so that, in order to; (+ *indicative, or no verb*) as
utor	uti, usus sum	*verb 3rd dep*	use (+ *abl*)
utrum ... an	*indecl*	*adv*	whether ... or
uxor	uxoris	*noun f 3*	wife
vale	*pl* valete	*imperat*	goodbye! farewell!
validus	valida, validum	*adj*	strong
vehementer	*indecl*	*adv*	violently, loudly
veho	vehere, vexi, vectus	*verb 3rd*	carry
vendo	vendere, vendidi, venditus	*verb 3rd*	sell
venio	venire, veni	*verb 4th*	come
ventus	venti	*noun m 2*	wind
verbum	verbi	*noun n 2*	word
vereor	vereri, veritus sum	*verb 2nd dep*	fear, be afraid
vero	*indecl*	*adv*	indeed
verto	vertere, verti, versus	*verb 3rd*	turn
verus	vera, verum	*adj*	true, real
vester	vestra, vestrum	*adj*	your (of you *pl*), yours
vexi		(*perfect of* veho)	
via	viae	*noun f 1*	road, street, way
vici		(*perfect of* vinco)	
victor	victoris	*noun m 3*	victor, winner
victoria	victoriae	*noun f 1*	victory
victus	victa, victum	(*perfect passive participle of* vinco)	
video	videre, vidi, visus	*verb 2nd*	see
videor	videri, visus sum	*verb 2nd dep*	seem, appear
villa	villae	*noun f 1*	house, country villa
vinco	vincere, vici, victus	*verb 3rd*	conquer, win, be victorious
vinum	vini	*noun n 2*	wine
vir	viri	*noun n 2*	man, male
virtus	virtutis	*noun f 3*	courage
vis	*acc* vim, *abl* vi, *pl* vires	*noun f irreg*	force, *pl* strength, military forces
visus	visa, visum	(*perfect passive participle of* video)	
vita	vitae	*noun f 1*	life
vivo	vivere, vixi	*verb 3rd*	live, be alive
vivus	viva, vivum	*adj*	alive, living
vixi		(*perfect of* vivo)	
voco	vocare, vocavi, vocatus	*verb 1st*	call
volo	velle, volui	*verb irreg*	want
volvo	volvere, volvi, volutus	*verb 3rd*	turn
vos	vestrum	*pron*	you (*pl*)
vox	vocis	*noun f 3*	voice, shout
vulnero	vulnerare, vulneravi, vulneratus	*verb 1st*	wound, injure
vulnus	vulneris	*noun n 3*	wound
vultus	vultus	*noun f 4*	expression, face

Index